FOUR WARS:

How America's Neglected Infrastructure Is Stealing Your Future

Four Wars:

How America's Neglected Infrastructure Is Stealing Your Future

Copyright © 2011 by George Melvin Barney

FOUR WARS books may be ordered by contacting:
Merit Books
3548 Golfing Green Drive
Farmers Branch, Texas 75234
www.mel-barney.com

ISBN: 978-0-9847614-2-5 (hc)
ISBN: 978-0-9847614-3-2 (sc)
ISBN: 978-1-4507-9469-5 (e)

Library of Congress CIP   20129334007

First Softcover Printing - June, 2012
Second Printing - October 2012
Printed in the United States of America

Edited by Kimberly Lausten
Cover and Book Design by Jeanne Ann Macejko

FOUR WARS

How America's Neglected Infrastructure Is Stealing Your Future

Mel Barney

MB

Merit Books

CONTENTS

MAXIMUM PRESIDENTIAL TAX RATES

YEAR	PRESIDENT		MAX. INCOME TAX RATE
1932	ROOSEVELT		70%
1945	TRUMAN		91%
1953	EISENHOWER		92%
1961	KENNEDY	83%	91%
1964	JOHNSON	Avg.	91%
1969	NIXON		79%
1974	FORD		79%
1977	CARTER		70%
1981	REAGAN		28%
1989	BUSH		31%
1993	CLINTON	33%	39%
2001	BUSH	Avg.	35%
2009	OBAMA		35%

INTRODUCTION

During my lifetime there have been four struggles that could have or may yet diminish the world power status of the United States. They are the Great Depression, World War II, the Cold War, and our present world economic crisis. I refer to each of these events as wars because both the Great Depression and our present world economic crisis center on the warfare between the very wealthy and the poor to middle class. This book is about my participation in these four wars, each of which involved class warfare. The message of the book is that the United States should be building trains not planes.

Key factors in the progress of the United States are taxes, expenditures, infrastructure, military spending, and shared sacrifice. These are the issues that I have observed through my life experiences and felt were most responsible for our country's declining economic status.

Our economic status as the world's greatest power started declining in the 1980's when our military spending increased and our infrastructure spending drastically decreased.

The maximum income tax rate under presidents Roosevelt through Carter varied between 70 to 91 percent. Starting with Reagan the maximum income tax rate was reduced to between 28 and 39 percent. Infrastructure expenditures peaked under Eisenhower at about 22 percent of Gross National Product (GNP) and then gradually decreased to about four percent of GNP under Reagan in the 1980s. It has since dropped to less than one percent in 2010. Military spending in the last fifty years has more than absorbed the funding we previously invested in infrastructure.

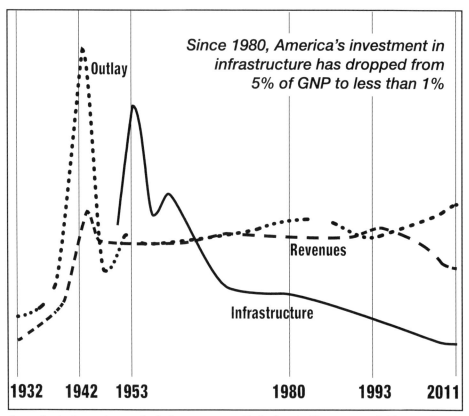

America's Investment in Infrastructure Relative to Revenues & Expenditures

I hope as you read *Four Wars* you will remember these trends that I believe have contributed to the current precarious economic climate. My direct participation, interest and observations in the four struggles provided me with the background to draw the important conclusions espoused in *Four Wars*.

My family was a political family and I had an unpleasant childhood until I got to the sixth grade. Fortunately Miss Greer, my sixth grade teacher, gave me a sense of self-worth and confidence that changed my whole outlook on life. I also had an eighth grade civics teacher who required that we read the editorial page every day and report on one issue. I still read the editorial page almost daily.

My professional career was a dream career doing what I loved to do. I invented, developed, and marketed mostly highly classified military weapons of war. I worked for Texas Instruments (TI) and had close contact with the local Central Intelligence Agency (CIA) Dallas agent for a period from 1963 until 1985.

My travels took me to fifty-four countries and included secret trips to Russia during the Cold War when citizens of the United States could not get a visa to travel to Russia. These trips supported the Brezhnev/Nixon détente initiative. The result of these trips was the start of a technology exchange between Russia and the United States that ultimately helped end the Cold War.

Four Wars provides my opinions as a member of Tom Brokaw's *Greatest Generation* on how we beat the Great Depression, won World War II, won the Cold War, and how the boomers are losing ground in the present world economic crisis.

Four Wars includes stories of my experiences being kidnaped in Lagos, Nigeria, shot at in Jakarta, Indonesia, having my life preserver get hung up on an anchor tossed into the Mississippi River, waking up with a gorilla in my bedroom, having one of two engines blow up at an altitude of 200 feet over the Appalachian Mountains, and many other experiences during my very active lifetime.

PART I

THE GREAT DEPRESSION
(1930-1941)

POLITICAL CLIMATE

THE GREAT DEPRESSION is considered by younger generations as just bad economic times, but many of us who lived through the period from the 1930s until 1941 will tell you personal stories of political and economic warfare. A small and very wealthy group was fighting to maintain the status quo while the shrinking middle class and poor were fighting for more good jobs and greater prosperity.

The United States was fortunate to have Roosevelt as a leader during the rough Depression period. He exuded confidence and had specific ideas that assured everyone we could survive this difficult time. He conducted talks on the radio, which he called fireside chats, to discuss specific programs the government was implementing. The Civilian Conservation Corps (CCC), the Works Progress Administration, the Tennessee Valley Administration (TVA), and

1

others were government initiatives that promised work and sound investment for the country. They have all returned their initial cost many times over through the years.

Most fathers and mothers at that time had no college education and many did not even have high school diplomas. Several of these parents, like mine, preached to their children that they must get a college education. Often the parents could not afford that education and had to find a way to pay. My family's plan was to prepare all three boys to be good enough at playing football to earn college football scholarships. In fact, that is what happened.

Winning a college scholarship was my primary goal during grammar and high school. My mother, who had attended college for two years, always insisted that we children go to college even though there was no money for it. Although my dad always had a job, we struggled financially, which created much family stress. My dad and my older brother were on one side of most family conflicts and my mother and I were on the other (weaker) side.

I had many boyhood jobs, including working in a chair factory when I was fourteen years old for fifteen cents an hour. The tight economic times put so much stress between my parents that, years later, they eventually divorced. This economic stress reached beyond the husband and wife to the children.

Most of those in the Greatest Generation age category still remember the champions that helped improve the conditions for the middle class and poor. Franklin Roosevelt and Huey Long were considered heroes by many.

I do not know what the outcome of the Great Depression would have been if the Japanese had not attacked Pearl Harbor and caused the United States to join the Allies to fight World War II. The wartime spending, military draft, and the inspired leadership of Roosevelt ended the Great

Depression shortly after December 7, 1941. With the draft, war tax, and Axis threat, all of our citizens had "skin in the game." The voters understood the precarious situation the country was in and forced the politicians to stop bickering and mobilize to win the war.

GROWING UP – ROCKY START

One of my early memories is the few days I spent in kindergarten in 1933. I was five years old. I was a sickly child and had many respiratory problems. My mother, in an effort to prevent colds, made mo wear socks that extended above my knees. The other children were unfriendly and started calling me "Lady Stockings." After a few days I managed to opt out of kindergarten.

I had developed extremely low self-esteem. This problem was a result of several situations I was experiencing. I had an older brother, Charlie, who my dad adored. Charlie treated me like a nuisance and, at two-and-a-half years my senior, insisted on calling me "Baby." Dad spent a lot of time with him and paid no attention to me. I was told later by my cousins that when I was born Dad had wanted a baby girl, not a boy. When we went on car trips, I would ask questions and Dad would order me to stop asking questions.

My boyhood home was at 2615 Coral Street in Shreveport, Louisiana. Our house was a two bedroom, one bath tract house in the western part of town. It was built in 1926 and cost about $1,000. Today if you drive on Interstate 20 about one mile east of the Independence Bowl Stadium, you will pass over the site where the house stood. When the Interstate Highway was built, they took my mother's home by exercising eminent domain. Her settlement for the home was below market price.

Mel Barney

In the mid 1930s, my dad installed an attic fan. This was a real treat during the hot Shreveport summers. He was always warning us not to close all of the windows or doors, because the fan would suck the wall paper off of the walls. My brother Charlie and I slept in the bedroom at the back of the house.

GORILLA IN MY BEDROOM

When I was eight, one morning I woke up and found myself staring into the eyes of what I thought was a white gorilla. He was about three feet in front of me making faces and giving me all kinds of hand signals. I screamed "Daddy, Daddy, Daddy!" My dad always slept with a pistol under his pillow. He was there almost immediately, pistol in hand. The gorilla made a few faces at dad and scampered out of the back screen door where he had entered the house.

We followed the trail of the intruder to the kitchen where he had gotten into the flour bin and covered himself and the kitchen with flour. We then followed his trail through the dining room and living room. He must have played on my dad's suit because the suit was all crumpled up and covered in white flour. After a little investigation, we determined that the neighbor directly across the alley kept a very large monkey in a cage behind his house. The monkey had gotten out of his cage and entered our house by tearing the screen out of our back door. I think in all of my life I have never been as terrified as when I woke up with that white gorilla making faces at me.

PUSH-PULLS AND OVALS

I entered grammar school and managed to pass first grade. In second grade, my teacher was Miss Tillitson. She had a reputation for being the strictest teacher in the school. By this time I had developed a negative attitude about life. I did not like her and she did not like me. I rebelled against several of her teaching methods. Typically, in the second grade, the writing lessons started with the class doing push-pulls and ovals. She was intent upon all students making ovals that were the same size around. The push-pulls had to be even at the top and bottom. I insisted on using my eraser to even the tops and bottoms of the push-pulls, which made sense to me. That was just one of many conflicts that I had with Miss Tillitson. She failed me, and I had to repeat the second grade. This was just one more setback for my ego.

My next second grade teacher was Miss Hatfield. She was very kind and gave me special attention. My ego began to improve. I began to realize that the most important opinion about me was the one I had of myself. I developed an attitude that I should do what I thought was right and not be concerned with other people's opinions of me.

HUEY LONG

At that time, the assassination of Louisiana Senator Huey Long had a big effect on me. He was shot down in 1935 on the steps of the Louisiana State Capital Building. I remember walking down Coral Street and seeing neighbors sitting on their porch swings and unashamedly crying because he had meant so much to them. The loss was a big blow to my parents, who adored Huey and touted his praises.

5

Louisiana in the 1920s had been about as corrupt as a state could be. Huey Long came along in 1928 promising reform and was elected governor by the highest percentage majority in the state's history. Huey removed the benefits enjoyed by the wealthy in terms of low taxes and rigged contract awards. He made the big oil companies pay the state, as well as land and royalty owners, a fair price for their mineral rights. He lowered taxes for the middle class, provided services to the poor, built roads and bridges, and improved the educational system. Like my parents, most of the middle class and poor idolized Huey, or "Kingfish," as he was called.

MATH, SOLUTION TO MY EGO PROBLEM

When I reached sixth grade, I had a wonderful teacher named Miss Greer. I had developed strong skills in math and she purposely had math exercises where she would state a problem then wait to see who could answer first. I was almost always first, which built my confidence. Even at my Claiborne Grammar Class school reunion in 2010, Evelyn Sikes, who was one of the prettiest girls in our class, commented that what she remembered most about me was that I was always the first to answer those math questions.

By the time I reached seventh grade, my failure in second grade was paying big rewards. I was the biggest and most mature student in the class. Also, I did extremely well in math and science. I was selected to make a puppet to play the part of Doc in our papier mache puppet show of Snow White and the Seven Dwarfs. I was also selected to play the leading role of Snoopy Crain, the great detective, in our seventh grade play The Haunted Tea Room.

MY MOTHER

My mother was good to me, but she had many stresses from conditions of the Depression and her rocky marriage. She attended most of my extracurricular activities. She loved me and always did her best for me.

OLDER BROTHER CHARLIE

During adolescence, I was not close to my brother Charlie. We were not even friends. He kept calling me Baby and I kept calling him Bubba. Dad took him to shooting matches, set up special physical training programs for him, and got him involved in scouting.

When I was about nine, mother left Charlie to take care of me for a few hours while she went to visit a friend. Charlie and I had an argument and I stuck my tongue out at him. He then gave me a hard upper cut, which severed about one inch of the middle of my tongue. My tongue was only connected by small portions on either side, but healed without any lasting problems. At that point, I realized I was in competition with Charlie.

Another notable event between Charlie and me was when our brother Harvey was born. I was twelve then and Charlie was taking care of me. We were sitting on the porch swing. Charlie was holding a nickel. He told me to hold my head back and open my mouth.

"You'll drop that nickel in my mouth," I protested.

"No, I won't," he assured me.

We argued for a while till I finally agreed. I held my head back and opened my mouth. Sure enough, he dropped the nickel into my mouth. It went down my throat and we never were able to recover it. This event instilled a trust-but-verify instinct in me.

I am proud to say that my younger brother Harvey has told me that I was a good big brother. He recounts times when my friends and I would play with him. I got him into playing football and golf, and spent time with him making things. After we grew up Charlie and I remained good friends and loving brothers.

By the time I graduated from Claiborne Grammar School I had developed self-confidence. I thought I was liked by all of my grammar school classmates. When an election was held at Fair Park High School, my Claiborne classmates nominated me for president of the freshman class. They worked hard and I won the election.

I developed an attitude that pushed me to compete with older brother, Charlie. With Dad's encouragement, Charlie was a Boy Scout, attaining the rank of Life Scout. I joined the Boy Scouts, and worked until I won the coveted rank of Eagle Scout. This was the first time I had achieved a notable victory over Charlie. I also worked hard to beat Charlie academically. In my freshman year of college, I made better than a B average. Charlie finished his career as a successful oil man. I am proud of Charlie and also of my own career, although I did not achieve his level of financial success

FATHER SON RELATIONSHIP

During the eight year period that I played football in high school and college, my dad attended few, if any, of my games. He attended all of Charlie's games in high school and many of his LSU games in Baton Rouge. Our relations were difficult to say the least.

During high school and college, I witnessed several inappropriate events that Dad was involved in. While a senior at Louisiana Tech, I was on a date with Carolyn, who later became my wife. We pulled up to the popular drive-in restaurant, Chat and Chew, in west Shreveport for hamburgers. I was shocked to see Dad and a young woman in the car next to us. Not thinking about the gun Dad carried, I jumped out, walked over and slapped him in the face. He made a speedy retreat. I loved my mother and hated to see her get hurt. Later, while still at Louisiana Tech, I was summoned to the divorce trial between my parents. I was asked to and did recount these incidents. I have always regretted that I did not have a better relationship with my dad.

Mel Barney

PART II

PREPARATION FOR WORLD WAR II (1940-1945)

1942: THE AMAZING YEAR

MANY OF US REMEMBER 1942. It was an amazing year. By then, our country had moved from the Great Depression to being the most powerful industrial nation in the world. The government's actions in this year vaulted the nation into superpower status that lasted for the next forty years. The key to this wonderful transition was the shared sacrifice that was imposed upon all citizens.

In 1940 the United States was supplying weapons to Great Britain and Russia. German submarines were sinking American merchant vessels in the Atlantic Ocean, and most of Europe, including France, had been invaded by Germany. A draft of men between the ages of 18 and 38 had started. In the Pacific Ocean, Japan was festering over the help the United States was providing to Chiang Kai-shek in China in support of its war against Japan. General Claire Chennault was leading a group of mercenary United States pilots operating out of China in the Chinese air war against Japan.

In September of 1940, President Roosevelt was advised by our Ambassador to Japan, Joseph Grew, that it was futile to try to negotiate with the Japanese.

Roosevelt then stopped all oil and scrap metal deliveries from the United States to Japan. By December of that year, Roosevelt commented in his fireside chat that our country must become the arsenal of democracy. Our government started the massive build up of weapons for the Allied nations. Many Americans did not really accept this war-oriented posture until the attack by the Japanese.

PEARL HARBOR

Before December 7, 1941, few people in the country had ever heard of Pearl Harbor. The attack by the Japanese was so sudden and destructive that the country was eager to retaliate. Anyone who did not rally around the flag was branded as unpatriotic. Roosevelt used this national fervor to pursue many smart initiatives to win the war, like extending the service period by those first drafted by the 1940 Selective Service Act and setting up a war tax to pay for the war. He also instituted a program to prevent profiteering by the weapons providers, began selling war bonds, recruited women to work in factories, and took many other actions to rally citizens behind the war effort.

Ultimately ten million (mostly men) were in service, out of a population of one hundred and twenty five million.

Young adults, like me, were allowed to do jobs normally reserved for older people. At age 16, I drove a truck with high octane gasoline to refuel fighter aircraft. I also drove an 18 wheeler for a produce company.

Our country did an amazing job. From December 7, 1941, until September 2, 1945, the country mobilized, won the war, and became the lone world superpower. These achievements make a strong case for the brilliance of our leaders at the time.

The decade that followed World War II was also characterized by brilliant leadership. Truman and Eisenhower provided college educations for returning servicemen, rebuilt Europe and Germany, and made significant improvements to America's infrastructure.

FAIR PARK HIGH SCHOOL

I attended high school during the war years. Everything was rationed, including gasoline, cars, shoes, and food. There were many jobs available to high school students during the summer. Many citizens for the first time in their lives had money to spend, though often what they wanted to spend it on was rationed, and thus not available.

In Shreveport then, the main sport was high school football. Dad had provided Charlie with many physical training opportunities like weight lifting and boxing which helped Charlie win a starting position on the Fair Park football squad. He won a football scholarship to Louisiana State University (LSU). In 1944 he entered the Navy. After returning to LSU in 1946 he continued playing football for the school. He played in three LSU post-season bowl games while earning a degree in petroleum engineering.

Charlie's accomplishments in football and college set

the bar pretty high for me. To make the Fair Park football team was a challenge. The two weeks of training before school started included two practices a day lasting two hours each. The practices were held in the humid late August Shreveport heat. No water was permitted on the practice field. More than one hundred players usually tried out for the team. By the end of the two weeks, the heat and coaches would pare this number down to forty players. In remembering these times, I wonder how the players endured these practices without having heat strokes. My good buddy Leo and I were thrilled when we got to college and discovered that those coaches provided cool water on the field for all practices.

During my first high school football fall training, there were many times that I thought I could not make it through the rigorous practice sessions. I would pull myself together and think if Charlie could do it, then I could do it too.

I was very active in high school. I had several different sweethearts, was elected to be president of several popular organizations, and was selected to represent Fair Park at the annual Pelican Boys State meeting in Baton Rouge. I also attained the rank of Major in the ROTC and was elected co-captain of the football team.

DRIVING A FLAMING GASOLINE TRUCK

The manpower shortage during World War II was so severe that both young and old were allowed to do jobs that would not normally be available to them. At sixteen, in 1944, I got a job fueling aircraft at the Shreveport Municipal Airport. The city hired another teenager and me to drive a gasoline truck and fuel Grumman F2Fs (Wildcats) and F4Fs (Hellcats). These two Navy fighter aircraft were being ferried from the Grumman aircraft plant in Bethpage Long Island, New York to the West Coast to fight in the Pacific war. My partner and I were both extremely cautious because of the danger of working with high-octane fuel.

One hot day we were returning to the fueling hanger on an open stretch of taxiway. I was driving. Out of nowhere, we heard a loud explosion. We looked back through the cab window and saw nothing but what looked to be white smoke. I jumped out of my side and he jumped out of his. I ran about 15 steps and hit the ground, expecting to be engulfed in flames any second. When I looked up, the gas truck was creeping down the taxiway. I could see a fire extinguisher blowing out white foam all over the cab of the truck. I got up and ran and jumped on the gas truck to stop it. I was glad when the summer was over and I no longer had to drive that gasoline truck.

During that summer, I spent some of my earnings learning to fly and got a student flight license. This required eight hours of lessons with a flight instructor and it allowed me to fly solo. I enjoyed the lessons, except for the final test when I was required to pull the airplane out of a tail spin, which sounded scary. It turned out to be easy though, as all I had to do was point the nose down and the airplane righted.

NEAR DISASTROUS TAKEOFF

I had two cousins who lived in Bethany, Texas, just twenty miles west of Shreveport. Bethany had about 300 residents. Bethany is half in Louisiana and half in Texas. My cousins were several years younger than me. I visited them often, as all during my childhood we were close friends. When I told them about my student pilot's license, they wanted me to land my airplane in the field behind their homes. We looked at the field and it appeared to be a satisfactory landing strip. I told them if they would cut the weeds in a path long enough to land, then I would land my airplane on the field. With help from others they cut the weeds. I inspected the site and told them I would call before I flew out. A few days later, I made the call and told them to expect me in about two hours.

My good friend Robert Tillery, had just received his student pilot's license. I had asked him if he would like to follow me in his airplane and land on the strip. He'd said he would. We flew out and made a flyover of the landing strip. Robert waved from his airplane indicating that he did not want to land. He turned back for home.

There were about twenty people waiting to watch the first airplane landing at Bethany. I did not want to disappoint them, so I came in for the landing low and slow. At first touchdown the airplane started shaking wildly. I stopped the roll and taxied over to the people. By the time I stopped I realized that the landing strip was in a field that had been an old cotton field. The rows ran crosswise to the landing strip direction. Although they were leveled considerably they still created resistance to the takeoff and landing speed.

I had bought my girlfriend a pretty bracelet and showed it off to my grandmother, aunts, and cousins. After a short visit, I had my cousin Billy get in the airplane and showed him how to turn the ignition on and off. I told him to leave it in the off position until I yelled contact, then to turn the ignition on. I also told him to hold the brakes down hard and push the throttle slightly forward when the engine started. My grandmother and aunts were horrified and did not want Billy to get into the airplane. I finally convinced them that it was safe and that I could not take off unless I had someone perform this function.

On an earlier visit I had roughly measured the take-off distance, which took into account the tall trees on both ends of the landing strip, and assumed a calm wind. I figured that I had several hundred extra feet over the needed distance. What I had not counted on was the crossways old cotton rows that covered the landing strip. I was concerned that the cotton rows would slow the take off, and considered not taking off, but would then have had too many questions to answer for landing on this strip in the first place.

With Billy in the cockpit and the ignition switched off, I cranked the engine several times to prime it. I then yelled "Contact" as I gave the propeller a hard spin. The engine started on the first try. I replaced Billy in the cockpit, waved at the people gathered to witness this event and taxied as far to the west end of the air strip as I could.

I revved the engine and released the brakes. The airplane slowly started its bumpy roll down the airstrip. After a few seconds, I became alarmed and started to abort the takeoff. However, by then the airplane was beginning to moderately accelerate. I was able to get the airspeed up to about 40 mph and the lift had eliminated most of the bumpy takeoff roll. I then started looking at the trees at the end of the airstrip. I was climbing at an airspeed of about 50 mph which was barely above stall speed. The trees became closer and closer. Finally I cleared the trees by not more than ten feet. From that day on, my cousins kidded me about my opening of the "Bethany International Airport."

HIGH SCHOOL SUMMERTIME ADVENTURES

One summer I went on two adventures along with my best friends: Leo Sanford, Kenneth Edwards, Ted Cole, and

Perry Montgomery. We went to Monterrey, Mexico in a Jeep, and took a hitchhiking trip to several states. My other trip during my high school years was to Hollywood, California.

During August 1945, Leo, Ted Cole, Loxla Stayton, Bill Doss and I hitchhiked from Shreveport to Dallas to Oklahoma City to Fort Smith and then to Shreveport. We happened to be in Dallas on August 14. This was V-J Day, the end of the war with Japan. Dallas had a huge celebration in front of the Adolphus Hotel, which we joined in on.

The next day we headed to Oklahoma City. We thought it would be fun to hop a freight train. We went to the rail yard and climbed into an empty boxcar that appeared to be heading north. After riding up and down the rail yard for several hours we decided to go back to hitchhiking.

After exploring Oklahoma City for several days, we headed to Fort Smith. All five of us were standing on the highway together. We usually split up because drivers did not like to pick up five guys at a time. A man and his wife driving a big Cadillac stopped to pick up all of us. After introducing his wife, he introduced himself as "Hoy the Boy," former governor of Oklahoma. Leo sat in the front right seat with Hoy and his wife, and the four of us sat in the back. As we drove along, Hoy was bragging about all of his accomplishments both political and physical. We explained that we all played high school football. Hoy got excited and all of a sudden, he let go of the steering wheel and reached across his wife and grabbed Leo by the neck.

He said, "Look here big boy. If I wanted to, I could take you out of the car and tear you from limb to limb."

Hoy's wife grabbed the steering wheel, Hoy released Leo, and we asked "Hoy the Boy" to let us out at the next town. We had a nice visit in Ft. Smith and hitchhiked back to Shreveport.

Later that summer, Leo and I, along with Kenneth Edwards, Perry Montgomery, and Ted Cole took off to Monterey, Mexico in Perry Montgomery's jeep. Our intent was to see the sights of Monterey, including Horse Tails Falls.

We all carried money enough to see the sights and return to Shreveport. We had planned carefully to make sure we had enough gas, motel, and food money, with some spare change. We figured the Jeep would get about 16 miles per gallon. By the time we got to Monterey, we discovered that at 75 miles an hour, a Jeep loaded down with five heavy people, only got about eight miles per gallon. It had taken practically all of our gasoline money to travel one way. We knew immediately that we were in money trouble, so we went to the American Consulate to see if they would allow us to contact our parents to send more money. The consulate was rude to us, and did not even allow us to enter the building. We spent several days in a cheap motel, five in the room and ate little.

There was a large Park in the middle of Monterey with a bandstand in the middle. In the evenings, a band would play Mexican music and many Mexicans would show up to enjoy the music. We noted that the young ladies and some with their parents would walk around the square clockwise on the inside and the young men with their parents would walk around on the outside in a counterclockwise direction. As the music played and time progressed we noted that many of the young men would join the young ladies in walking around the park in a clockwise direction. Our group decided to join the young men walking around the park in the counterclockwise direction. However, none of us were ever able to decipher the code that would allow us to join the young women walking the opposite way.

After a few days of sightseeing with little money to spend, we decided to head back to Shreveport. We were within about 70 miles of the border and saw a Mexican cantina by the side of the road. We were thirsty, so we decided to stop and have a soda. As we were sitting there drinking our soda pop we heard a gunshot. Then we saw a little man come running through the cantina followed by a large man with a six-shooter.

The large man was shouting, "So you're the S. O. B. who's been messing around with my wife." Shooting about every three seconds, but missing the little man.

We all ran for the door, windows or whatever we could find to get out of the cantina and back into the Jeep. As we drove off, we heard all of the locals laughing at us.

When we got to within about 20 miles of the Texas border, we had a blowout. We had already had one blowout on this Jeep and had no more spare tires, so we rimmed it all the way back to the border. Fortunately, Leo had an uncle in the Texas border city who gave us enough money to return to Shreveport.

In the summer of 1945, my girlfriend's friend's mother wanted to take her daughter and her friend to Hollywood to audition for movie roles. The two girls were beautiful and excellent tap dancers. The mother had set up movie tryouts for the two girls. Fortunately the girls' boyfriends, Ted Cole and I, were invited to go on the trip.

We had a wonderful week in Hollywood, and saw many of the famous tourist attractions of Los Angeles. The highlight of the trip was an evening at the Palladium Ballroom. I remember the band that played that night being the famous Frankie Carl Band. The trip went off as planned and everyone had a truly great time, though the two girls did not get any offers for the movies.

During my junior and senior year in high school I had a steady girl friend. I was in love with her and I thought she was in love with me. When she realized I planned to get a college degree before marriage, or for some other reason, she broke off the relationship. I went off to Louisiana Tech and spent lonely weekends for several months.

SAINT GEORGE

I had a lot of close friends in high school. Sometimes they would get into more mischief than I was willing to tolerate. On Halloween they were particularly creative. They would do things such as pulling the rod on top of the streetcar off of the power wire above when the streetcar stopped to pick up someone. The streetcar operator would have to get out and reconnect the top rod to the wire. When they started this kind of behavior I would go home. On one occasion the police caught them after I had gone home. They had to go to court and pay a fine. As a result of my actions they started calling me Saint George.

LOUISIANA TECH

After football season ended in my senior year at Fair Park High School, several of the top prospects for playing college football were invited to visit colleges interested in their attendance at these colleges. I was fortunate enough to be in this group. We were provided transportation to these colleges. We talked to the coaches and were shown the athletic facilities. The coaches would describe their training programs and discuss their hopes for building winning teams and our chances for getting starting positions on them. They discussed former players who had succeeded in the National Football League. We were escorted around the campuses by girls who attended the colleges and were set up on blind dates with college girls.

LEO

During high school and college, my best friend was Leo Sanford. Leo was six feet two inches tall and solidly built. He played center on the football teams and I played right guard. We went on double-dates with our girlfriends all through high school. After graduation, he went to Louisiana Tech, and I planned to go to LSU where my brother was enrolled. Before enrolling at LSU, I was contacted by a coach from the University of Florida who invited Leo and me to come and play there. I called Leo and he suggested that before we go to Florida, I visit Louisiana Tech. I agreed and met Leo and Coach Mize (La. Tech line coach) in Shreveport. After visiting Tech, I decided to play football there instead of LSU. Tech had a good football program and a highly regarded engineering school.

When Leo graduated college he was drafted by the Chicago Cardinals. He played several years for them and then was traded to the Baltimore Colts. This was during the Johnny Unitas era. The Colts were one of the best NFL teams. Leo has a Super Bowl ring from the 1958 Super Bowl when the Colts beat the New York Giants in overtime. This was the first Super Bowl that was telecast throughout the world. He also played in two Pro Bowls. He then returned to Shreveport where he obtained the multi-state franchise for a major cap, gown, and senior ring franchise. Leo is a very likeable gentleman and has been successful in this business.

I had enjoyed high school and looked forward to the same at Louisiana Tech. During my high school years, my older brother Charlie was in the service and I had few activities that included my dad. My younger brother Harvey was twelve years younger and we had few areas of mutual interest. In retrospect, I feel a bit of guilt that I did not take more interest in Harvey. When I went to Tech I did not miss being in Shreveport. I roomed with my best friend Leo. Leo went home each weekend to be with his beautiful girl friend, Myrna Mims. This gave me a lot of weekend time to do my homework.

I was determined to do well in my courses and I made three A's, two B's and one C during my first semester. During spring training, I realized that playing football and studying engineering required an exceptionally high level of discipline in order to do both well. During one month in the spring, football required four hours a day. It took this much time to time to travel to the practice field, put on your uniform and pads, practice for two hours, shower, dress, and return to your dormitory. We practiced five days a week. During the fall this routine lasted from mid August until early December, with an added five hours on Saturday when the games were played. In addition to the practice time, we had to memorize more than 50 plays.

During my first weeks of spring training in 1947, I felt that I had impressed the coaches with my quick and tough performance against the seasoned players. One experience that I will always remember is the drill that our head coach, Joe Aillet, set up for all of the team to watch. He had Coach Mize take Leo, who played center, and me to the middle of the field. Coach Mize set me up directly in front of Leo in the nose guard position. Leo outweighed me by 25 pounds. Coach gave Leo the ball and told him to snap it and not to let me get past. I was not to go around Leo. My tactics were to hit him head on as hard as I could, try to leap over him, fake left and go right, and submarine, which meant to go under him and rise up. Leo was tough and he probably won the battle, but I put everything I had into the drill.

When I enrolled at Louisiana Tech, I had two dominant objectives: to make good grades in the electrical engineering (EE) school and to work as hard as I could on the football field. If I did not perform on the football field, I could lose my scholarship. The first few months were really tough. I was taking rigorous engineering courses, my roommate, Leo, went home every weekend to see his future wife, Myrna, and I no longer had a girlfriend. I got into the habit of doing my homework the evening after attending the class. On the weekends I spent my time in the library or my room studying.

During our first spring football training, Leo and I were used mostly as blocking or tackling dummies. After spring training was over, I made my first trip back to Shreveport. I was bruised all over, with a black eye, sores on my face, and a sore knee. My mother was so alarmed that she tried to get me to quit football, but I had no intention of giving up football and losing my scholarship.

BEST COLLEGE LINEBACKER

In our freshman year before the regular season started, Coach Mize set up a game for the freshmen players to play a team from Barksdale Air Force Base. I was playing nose guard and Leo was playing middle linebacker. I told Leo I was having a great time with the Barksdale offensive center, and Leo said "Let me have a crack at him."

I agreed, so Leo took the nose guard position and I took middle linebacker. Their quarterback, an experienced college football player named Sparky Watts, took the snap from the center and dropped back to pass. His right end drifted right and I moved to my left. Sparky threw the ball to the right end. I moved in front of him and caught the ball. I ran 55 yards for the touchdown. We won the game 6 to 0. Since I only played linebacker for that one play, I have to have the best linebacker statistics in college football.

NICE MOVEMENT MEL

During our first spring training, coach Aillet would frequently run a play and comment to all, "Nice movement, Mel," meaning me. My friends had always called me either George or Melvin. Coach Aillet's comment stuck and my teammates would tease me, repeating "Nice movement, Mel." The name Mel has stuck ever since.

ECONOMICS - COLLEGE ATHLETE 1949

Typically during fall football season I took 12 or 13 course hours. In the spring I would take 17 or 18 hours. I went to summer school three years and made up the hours I got behind each fall. The total time I spent training, and playing college football was about 515 hours for nine months. The scholarship provided me about seventy-five dollars per month in college expenses. For nine months this comes to $675. I was pleased with my situation and have no complaints. I got an education that I would never have gotten without football.

UNWANTED PUBLICITY

I had a goal of playing in the NFL. Any publicity on the national sports pages improved your chances of being identified by the NFL scouts. I worked hard on the football field and made the starting lineup as a sophomore. One of my biggest football assets was quickness. The starting lineup played both offense and defense. During the fourth quarter of a mid season game, the coach took me out to rest for a few plays. I was standing on the sidelines and the opponent ran a play directly where I was standing. The runner fumbled the ball and it rolled off of the field right at my feet. Instinctively, I covered the ball. One of the major news wires picked up on the story and the next day sports papers all over the country were reporting that Melvin Barney, a substitute guard for La. Tech had jumped off of the bench and covered an opponent's fumble. I had worked so hard to make the starting lineup, and this was a blow to my ego. Even today some of my old friends remind me of this move.

Game ball awarded by our Louisiana Tech coaches for my performance during the first game in my senior year

The student council was planning an event to build campus spirit for our football team which was having a great year. The event would be called the powder puff derby, and would feature a football game with only women on the teams. The women players included many of the girlfriends of the varsity team. My girlfriend, Carolyn was picked to replicate the event where I had covered the football on the sideline. She tried to get out of this spoof but the planners finally convinced her to do it, to promote team spirit. I am not winning any accolades from her for including this story in this book.

I thoroughly enjoyed my years of playing football. Leo was always on my left side when we lined up for a play. I was fortunate to have outstanding coaches in both high school and college. In fact, during my sophomore year at La. Tech, my coach had me teaching the techniques that I had learned in high school to the freshmen players.

ONE HALF VETS AND ONE HALF NON-VETS

There was a wonderful uniting spirit on our team, between the war veterans and the younger non-veterans. Though I had been too young to serve in World War II, I was proud to be admitted into the National Guard, where I served from 1948 through 1950. Coach Aillet had promised all players going off to war that there would be an athletic scholarship waiting for them when they returned. The veterans had a special empathy for the younger players who had not had the direct exposure to the war that they had. That team spirit lives on through today. The 45 members of our Tech football team along with our four coaches have had annual meetings, including wives, every year since graduation. We named this group the Organization of the Louisiana Tech football team graduates - 1947-1950. We have self-appointed presidents, secretaries, treasurers, a poet laureate, and program chairmen.

We meet every year to play golf and tell tales about our heroics on the gridiron. We always select the "Horse's Ass" (really an honor) for the year. The highlight of these meetings is the reading by an original NAAGQ poem by our own poet laureate, Sese Holstead. One of her inspirational poems appears in the appendix. In 2011 we had 15 players from the original squad and one coach at our meeting. Our line coach Jimmy Mize, who is 94 years old, and his wife Minnie were there.

LEE HEDGES   MELVIN BARNEY   COACHES
CO-CAPTAINS   FAIR PARK H. S. 1946
CO-CAPTAINS   LA. TECH 1950
LEO SANFORD   MELVIN BARNEY

I was elected by my teammates to be co-captain of both my high school and college football teams. Both of my co-captains, Lee Hedges (high school) and Leo Sanford (college) were inducted into the Louisiana Sports Hall of Fame.

CAROLYN

During my first semester at La. Tech, a good friend, Nappy Baird, was a sophomore working on an electrical engineering degree. Realizing I was lonely, he introduced me to Carolyn. I was instantly mesmerized by Carolyn's demeanor and beauty. I called my mother that night and told her that I had met the girl I was going to marry. That goal became my third dominant objective. It proved as difficult to achieve as the first two.

Carolyn in her college years

Carolyn was popular, a good student, and a class officer. She was selected as both the all campus beauty and homecoming queen. Though I was a good student and was elected to several class office positions, the only financial resource I had was my scholarship, which covered all of my books, tuition, room, board, and ten dollars per month for social and other needs. In spite of some tough competition, I started going steady with Carolyn during my junior year. We married on June 2, 1950, and celebrated our sixty-first anniversary on June 2, 2011. I will forever be indebted to Leo for influencing me to go to La. Tech where I met my wife, lover, mother of my children, and best friend: Carolyn.

ACADEMICS

I studied hard and only had trouble in two subjects. One was chemistry, which I had not had in high school. I eked out Cs for the eight hours of chemistry I was required to take. The other subject was psychology, the only elective I took in my electrical engineering curriculum. The course was nothing like I had expected. Today I could not tell you what the course was all about. The only thing I can confirm is that I barely managed to pass it with a D.

MY FIRST AND LAST SOLO AT TECH

One of the favorite professors at Tech was Dr. Sachs. He taught literature. I liked his class but he required us to memorize many lines of poetry, which took a lot of time. I was always pressed for time.

My favorite of all the required poems was William Ernest Henley's "Invictus". The last verse of the poem reads:

It matters not how strait the gate,
How charged the punishment the scroll,
I am the master of my fate,
I am the captain of my soul.

This verse reminded me of many challenges I had already faced in my life. It gave me confidence that I could accomplish difficult goals. I always carry a copy in my billfold. The entire poem appears in the appendix.

During one of his classes, Dr. Sachs offered to give credit for learning 50 lines of poetry to anyone who would learn the words to the English song "Drink to Me Only with Thine Eyes" and sing it in the next class meeting. I was the only one who raised his hand.

He warned, "Be ready to sing it during the next class period, Mr. Barney."

During the next class, Dr. Sachs said, "Alright, Mr. Barney, you are on."

As soon as I started to sing, Dr. Sachs stopped me, saying, "That's enough Mr. Barney."

I have to admit that I was somewhat embarrassed, but the embarrassment was totally offset by the credit for remembering all of those lines. I think everyone who had Dr. Sachs knew he was a tough professor, but they enjoyed his classes.

IN RETROSPECT

Upon receiving my Bachelor of Science in Electrical Engineering Degree, I felt good about reaching the goal my mother had set for me so many years ago. However, there were so many stresses in terms of grades, football, campus activities, and constant lack of money that I look back and wonder how it would have been if I had more support from the outside. The determination required to achieve my graduation goal helped me to understand that perseverance is one of the most reliable tools for success.

PART III

COLD WAR
(1948-1991)

ELECTRICAL ENGINEERING
OR PRO FOOTBALL

IN 1950, Carolyn and I were married on June 2. She taught school that year while I finished my fourth year of engineering school and fourth year of college football. Upon graduation in May of 1951, I had several good job offers with companies such as Louisiana Power and Light and IBM. I also had an offer to try out for the Los Angeles Rams professional football team.

I loved playing football, had been doing it for eight years, and really wanted to go to the Rams try out. My buddy Leo had a firm offer to play for the Chicago Cardinals (now the Arizona Cardinals). But after watching many undersized and less talented football players try out for high school and college teams and not make it, I felt that I would be a blocking dummy for the Los Angeles Rams. I realized that

I was not likely to make it as a pro football player. Besides, I did not want to relinquish the great job opportunity with Sperry Gyroscope Company that I'd received.

SPERRY

I had a passion for flying and a student pilot's license. The job with Sperry would put me into the development of new aeronautical instruments for the most modern jet airplanes, so I accepted the job with Sperry. Carolyn and I packed all of our possessions into our new 1950 Ford and took off for New York City.

There were ten other engineers in my training group at Sperry, all from the Northeast. My southern accent made a big difference in the way I was accepted in the group. All but one or two of the engineers treated me as though I was something special. Each Monday morning as I came in to work, they would ask me what Carolyn and I had seen over the weekend. We had always been to landmarks like the Statue of Liberty, the Empire State building, Rockefeller Center, or Coney Island. Many of them had never visited any of these attractions.

The focus of our training was on the design and development of automatic pilots for high performance aircraft. We learned the basics of how the autopilot dynamics could be synergistically coupled with the aircraft dynamics to provide smooth flight.

HIGH ALTITUDE DECOMPRESSION

One of the assignments of Sperry's engineering training program was to experience high altitude decompression.

The reason was that many of the engineers would be flying on high altitude military aircraft. This training stressed what to do in case the aircraft lost pressurization at high altitude.

Six engineers at a time were taken to Roosevelt Field at the Grumman Aircraft facility on Long Island. The Grumman High Altitude Decompression Chamber was a steel circular chamber, which was similar to, yet bigger than, a railroad tanker car. It had a steel bulkhead between two compartments with a door between the two.

After a briefing on what to expect and what to do, we entered the chamber and were given pencils and tablets. We were given oxygen masks, but told not to use them. With the door between the two chambers closed, one of the two instructors told us to start writing the letters of the alphabet. The air in the other chamber was evacuated. One of the two instructors then took a small hammer and knocked out the glass plate that separated the two chambers. The air density in our chamber changed immediately from sea level to 35,000 feet as the chamber filled with a dense cloud which cleared quickly.

We concentrated on writing the alphabet. Some of us observed that the other engineers were writing their letters slower and slower. We felt no discomfort. When the engineers stopped writing the alphabet, the instructors put their oxygen masks on them and their alphabet writing speed returned to normal. The same thing happened to me but I did not remember slowing down my alphabet writing. I did not even realize that someone had put my oxygen mask on me. We all did remember that when you have decompression at high altitude, you must get your oxygen mask on as soon as possible.

The training was going well, however my salary of 270 dollars a month was insufficient to maintain an adequate living standard in New York City, which was very expensive at that time. My mother managed to get us a loan from a bank in Shreveport, which allowed me to finish my training in New York City.

At that time there was a severe housing shortage in New York. We finally found a six room unfurnished apartment in a high-rise. We put our card table, ironing board, two stools, and a radio in the apartment. We bought a Hollywood bed from Mister Feinstein's furniture store. The apartment was in Great Neck, Long Island and was close to the downtown shopping area so that Carolyn could get out of the apartment while I was at work.

While I was working one day, the Welcome Wagon lady showed up to welcome us to the neighborhood. Carolyn invited her into the apartment and invited her to have a cup of coffee. As they were chatting, the woman asked Carolyn when they were going to deliver our furniture. This comment, along with Carolyn's feelings of isolation during my days at training left her uncomfortable living in New York with little to do. The radio we had brought with us from Louisiana helped somewhat. Television was primitive then, and not within our budget.

Upon completing my training we moved to Wichita, Kansas. Here, Boeing was just getting started on their new B-47 jet bomber, for which Sperry was providing the bomb sight and automatic pilot.

FROM NEAR POVERTY TO RELATIVE WEALTH

Carolyn got a job teaching third grade. I had received a raise when I was moved to Wichita. I was working six days a week, mostly on the night shift, which paid a fifteen percent bonus, and making double time on every hour above

40. In addition to my salary of $350 per month, I received a relocation allowance of $160 for each of the first six months. We put away a certain amount of each paycheck for our furniture budget, and another we put into savings bonds. We also paid back the loan that my mother had gotten us from Shreveport.

A FUN JOB

My new job was extremely interesting. We were installing the first automatic pilots in the first prototype swept wing high speed jet bombers. My assignment was on the Sperry A-12 automatic pilot, a vacuum tube type of equipment. I had not heard of transistors then. The A-12 had sensors that included a vertical Gyro, a directional Gyro, and rate gyros orthogonally placed in the aircraft. These sensors proved to be inadequate to provide the necessary aerodynamic control of the aircraft. It wasn't until the Kearfott Schuler-tuned inertial platform was received in early 1952 that we were able to get the necessary sensor inputs to satisfactorily control the aircraft.

The XB-47 was the first jet powered swept winged high altitude bomber for the United States. It turned out to have some very strange aerodynamic characteristics. There were ten XB-47 prototypes built to test things like structure, avionics, and flight characteristics. Once the tests on the aircraft were successfully completed, the B-47 was put into full production.

The B-47

Of the ten XB-47 prototype aircraft built, there were many dangerous near-fatal and three fatal crashes. I witnessed one of these accidents and was told about the other two lost aircraft by my friends at Boeing. The one that I witnessed was the first experimental test to demonstrate the use of JATO (Jet Assisted Take Off). Rockets were placed on both sides of the XB-47 to add thrust for a short takeoff. The whole Boeing engineering staff was aware of the tests and located themselves in a position to watch the takeoff. Most of the Sperry engineers were also on hand to watch.

We watched as the XB-47 taxied out to the runway. It lined up on the takeoff runway and throttled up to full power on the six jet engines. The JATO rockets were fired and the aircraft accelerated rapidly. The aircraft was off the ground quickly. As it took off, you could see that it was yawing, or deviating laterally from the correct direction. It did not get very far off of the ground before it flipped over and crashed. Aviation Week magazine covered the crash investigation. The problem was that one side of the two JATO rockets put out more thrust than the other side, causing the fatal maneuver.

The other XB-47 crash involved two of these test aircraft. It happened a few months before we moved to Wichita. When one of the aircraft was landing, the test pilot noted that the landing gear down lock light did not come on when he lowered the landing gear. The second XB-47 then tried to fly below the troubled XB-47 to see if his crew could locate the problem. Reportedly, the slipstream of the troubled aircraft caused the other XB-47 to fly up into the troubled aircraft, resulting in the crash of both aircraft.

Boeing had one of these XB-47 test aircraft in a hanger to test the wing structure. Each day I went to work I would pass this hanger on my way to the Sperry Office. The aircraft sat upside down on a high platform. They would continually load the wings with heavy weights, adding weight until the wing finally broke. The aircraft specification was that the wings would support three times the weight of the fully loaded aircraft. The wing structure passed this test. When I flew with the crews on some of the test flights, I could see the substantial bowing of the wings as we negotiated a steep turn. Boeing engineers told me that the wings could bow up to ten feet before they would break.

The swept wings of this new aircraft caused a natural problem called Dutch roll. Dutch roll was caused by any deviation from the aircraft's heading directly into the air stream. With a heading shift, one wing would be more perpendicular to the air stream, causing that wing to produce more lift and in turn causing to bank in the opposite direction. One function of the automatic pilot was to control this tendency. In addition to the Dutch roll, the aircraft tended to porpoise, meaning to fly up and then down at a frequency of about 15 seconds per cycle. Its heading would try to go left then right at a frequency of about 30 seconds per cycle.

There was a dangerous coffin corner altitude at which the aircraft had a smaller and smaller range of safe airspeeds between high speed buffet and stall. This very dangerous problem started at about 35,000 feet of altitude and was highly dependent upon the load that the aircraft was carrying. This was particularly troublesome when the aircraft was refueled while in the air. The automatic pilot was needed to help the pilot with all of these problems.

BASICS OF AUTOMATIC PILOT DESIGN

An automatic pilot design requires an understanding of calculus. All three axes of heading, pitch, and roll must be controlled. Each of these axes requires sensor inputs that measure the deviation from a straight flight path, as well as the rate and acceleration of the deviation. When the characteristics of these sensors and the aircrafts dynamics are matched correctly, a smooth route to the desired flight path can be achieved.

The three automatic pilot sensors proved inadequate to satisfactorily control this new family of jet aircraft. Not until the Kearfott Laboratory Shuler tuned inertial platform was received in early 1952 were we able to get the necessary sensor inputs to satisfactorily control the aircraft.

I worked with the aeronautical stabilization engineers at Kearfott Laboratories on several projects including one at Texas Instruments. I do not understand the detailed dynamics of the Shuler tuned inertial platform, but I do know that this type of platform includes three gyros built to have a natural dynamic characteristic of a pendulum. With this natural dynamic, any movement of the platform does not cause the platform to lose its ability to sense the true vertical and directional position with respect to the earth.

During the early part of the flight test program, the test pilots would come back from a flight and be upset with the performance of the autopilot. They would ask for a Sperry engineer to accompany them and experience the problems first hand. I had told my boss that I liked making these flights. The B-47 had a place for a crew of three. If a fourth engineer flew on the test mission, he would sit in the crawlway seat to the pilots left and about a foot below the pilot's seat. The pilot and co-pilot had ejection seats that aimed upward. The navigator had an ejection seat that ejected downward. The fourth crew member was told in case the pilot chose to eject, the fourth crew member was to exit through the entrance hatch just behind his seat.

On one of the flights, the navigator station was not occupied and I was allowed to sit in the navigator's nose seat. When we took off, the cooling blower above me filled the navigator station with what I thought was smoke. I yelled into the microphone, "Mayday! Mayday! There is smoke in the navigator station."

The pilot came on the intercom and calmly said, "Keep your shirt on, that is just condensation." I asked him to advise me of anything that was different than what one would normally experience.

We were able to solve one problem in a strange way. The problem was a jitter in the rudder channel. It was not a serious flight problem but it annoyed the pilots. The sensors that feed flight information to the autopilot all have dead zones. A dead zone is a small part of the control sensor that is the center of the output signal. When in this zone the sensor sends no signal to the autopilot, and the autopilot does not sense which direction to move. We solved the problem by putting in a very small 400 cycles per second signal that was outside of the autopilot dynamics response capability. We called this fix a dither, and it was a technique used more than one time to fix problems in closed circuit control problems.

One problem with the automatic pilot was with the vertical gyro, which tells the system which way is up. It always sensed the apparent gravity vector to keep the gyro upright. When in a coordinated turn the apparent gravity shifts to the angle from vertical that the aircraft is banking. The liquid level will try to tilt the gyro off vertical during these turns. In a long continuous turn, the liquid level will cause the vertical gyro to point other than up. We solved the problem by cutting off the liquid level erection system during turns. The turning signal was provided by the heading gyro.

The problem was solved completely after we had received and incorporated the Kearfott Shuler tuned inertial platform. This platform is unaffected by the maneuvering of the aircraft. It was one of the most significant improvements to the dynamics of controlling modern day aircraft.

During the early part of the flight test program, the test pilots would come back from a flight and would insist that I get in the airplane with them to experience the problems they were having in-flight. We had a group of engineers in Wichita, and together we would analyze the problems with the automatic pilot. I would take the data from the flight test and go to New York and work with the Sperry engineers to resolve the problems. We were able to solve many of the problems by making changes to the system in Wichita.

I was enthusiastic and enjoyed this assignment. After a while I had developed very good relations with my counter parts at Boeing. From time to time the Boeing engineers would travel to Great Neck, Long Island to discuss problems directly with the autopilot engineers at Sperry. In addition to working on technical problems, I was considered the host, and was expected to entertain the Boeing visitors. I would take them to Broadway shows, restaurants, and other popular tourist attractions.

During World War II, the United States government built three mile-long aircraft production hangers. One was located in Fort Worth, Texas, one was located in Marietta, Georgia, and one was built in Tulsa, Oklahoma. When the decision was made to produce hundreds of B-47 bombers, the Air Force set up a production line in the Tulsa mile-long production hanger. In early 1953 we were moved to Tulsa to support the start up production of the B-47s in the mile-long hangar.

We got settled in Tulsa and on May 12th we were happy to welcome Barbara Anne, a beautiful baby girl, to our family. Barbara Anne was a caring, studious and inquisitive young girl. She retains all of those wonderful characteristics today. She has the beauty of her mother. She loved going to SMU and graduated with a BA degree in 1975. Later she received two more degrees from SMU. Barbara has a daughter, Natalie, who lives in central Texas.

Barbara has the ability to focus her energy on specific objectives and work until they are accomplished. She is a real estate agent in Dallas. The present real estate market would cause many to get discouraged, but she has had the tenacity and stamina to succeed in this competitive market. She has always been artistically inclined and even designed the floor plan and interior of the home we built in 1988.

Our son, George Michael, was born in Tulsa on August 6, 1955, and we were so glad to have a wonderful little boy. Mike was a gregarious, outgoing, caring child and is still that way today. Mike graduated from Texas Tech in 1978.

His career as an electrical engineer has been very similar to mine. He has traveled all over the world and his family has lived in South Korea and Saudi Arabia.

Mike and Kathy Weller married in 1978. They have four children, Elizabeth, Michael, Daniel, and Tyler. Mike was interested in Scouting and earned the rank of Eagle. He has served as scout master and has taken scouts to many annual outings at Philmont in Northern New Mexico. My Dad, Mike's sons Daniel and Tyler and I also earned the rank of Eagle Scout. That is four generations of Eagle Scouts.

AN AIRPORT WITH NO GASOLINE

The Douglas Engineers Club had a flying club. They asked me to join. I did and completed the requirements for a private pilot license. I had worked for my granddad while I was in high school, as a carpenter. He taught me a lot. For instance he instructed me to always "measure twice and cut once." He passed away in Shreveport. I wanted to go to his funeral, so I got permission to fly the club's Aero-Coupe to Shreveport.

This rudderless airplane had a butterfly tail and no rudder pedals. It was a rough airplane to fly in choppy weather. I filed a flight plan and then took off from Tulsa to Shreveport, a distance of approximately 260 miles. When I was about 70 miles from Shreveport, I noted the gasoline gauge was near empty. I looked at my chart and found an airport in my current vicinity. I rolled up to the gasoline pump and asked the attendant if I could fill up.

"Sorry fellow, but our tanks are empty, "He said, suggesting another airport about 15 miles away.

With a substantial amount of angst, I took off and made

it to the nearby airport. I attended my granddad's funeral, returned to the airport, and started my flight back to Tulsa. About halfway to Tulsa I ran into rain and low clouds. The weather seemed to get rougher and the clouds lower as I went. At times I flew for up to five seconds in clouds. I managed to get back to Tulsa safely, but resolved not to fly again until I could afford an IFR (Instrument Flight Rules) aircraft, and had an IFR License.

Tulsa is a fine city and we were one happy family. We had added two precious members to our family. In December 1955, most of the work at Douglas had been accomplished and Sperry moved me to Dallas, Texas.

DALLAS, ANOTHER FUN ASSIGNMENT

During the 1950s, there were many wealthy oil people in the North Texas area. They were buying executive aircraft and outfitting them with the most modern equipment. My job was to supervise the installation of this equipment and keep Sperry informed of any problems. I met many of the aircraft owners, and at times was invited to accompany them on trips, including some to their luxurious hideaways. In addition to the executive aircraft operations, I also monitored the Sperry equipment performance on American, Delta, and Braniff aircraft.

STALLING A DC-7

I was asked by Braniff Airlines to accompany their chief test pilot to Los Angeles to take delivery of their first DC-7 aircraft. Among other things, the Braniff chief test pilot wanted to test the Sperry automatic pilot. On our trip back to Dallas, the pilot wanted to see what the reaction of the autopilot would be in a stalled aircraft condition. With the automatic pilot engaged, he slowly pulled back on the throttles, being careful to keep symmetrical power on all four engines. He then waited for the aircraft to slow down below stall speed. The autopilot was trying to maintain level flight as the aircraft dropped. Although we were dropping like a rock, the aircraft maintained level wings and directional stability.

SAN ANTONIO FIASCO

Dee Howard in San Antonio, Texas was producing executive aircraft using a stretched version of the Lockheed Ventura bomber. He had added a ten-foot long section to the middle of the fuselage, had extended the mounts on the engines to counterbalance the additional weight in the tail section, and had added higher powered engines. He had selected the Sperry autopilot for this airplane. My job was to supervise the installation and make sure the performance was satisfactory.

During my last trip to San Antonio, I was to accompany an oil company's chief pilot and Dee Howard's crew on the acceptance flight for the airplane.

Our first test was to climb to a 10,000 foot altitude and test the dive brakes. Dee had put two large panels behind the engines on each side to be extended downward slowing the aircraft in case of a dive. During the first test, the chief pilot dove the airplane at a speed of 360 miles per hour, which was the plane's maximum air speed. The airplane shook violently, but slowed to a reasonable speed and the dive brakes were retracted.

One of the crew in the back hollered up to the pilot, "You

can't scare us. "

The chief pilot then started a second dive. This time he dove about 20 miles an hour above the maximum airspeed of the airplane. One dive brake extended and the other one did not. At this point, the aircraft was completely out of control upside down and spinning wildly.

None of the five people in the back were strapped in and we bounced around the cabin like ping-pong balls. After about 20 seconds, the pilot was able to return the aircraft to an upright position. Dee Howard was one of five passengers in the cabin. He told the pilot to land immediately. As we exited the aircraft, Dee asked when I could come back and finish the automatic pilot tests. I told Dee that I was headed back to Dallas and would not return. It took two martinis to get me on the airplane to Dallas.

Two weeks later I had to visit Sperry in New York City. I took a train all of the way from Dallas to New York City and back. It wasn't such a bad trip, but I decided that the best way to travel long distance was to fly.

OMNI STATION OOPS

While with Sperry, I would frequently be allowed in the cockpit of commercial airline flights to observe the Sperry equipment performance on that aircraft. After I left Sperry I would sometimes, out of curiosity, ask to visit the cockpit on a commercial flight. Most of the time, I would be allowed in the cockpit to observe equipment performance. That is no longer allowed. The experience discussed below resulted from one of these cockpit visits.

OMNI stations are electronic beacons that transmit in all directions. The signal sent out is a precise beam that identifies the precise direction to or from a specific OMNI station. Before GPS, this was the primary navigation system that allowed aircraft crews to know where they were. It did so by triangulating between two OMNI stations. This information told the pilot which direction to fly.

Before I left Sperry, the company was working on an improvement to the autopilot that would allow an autopilot that was flying the aircraft to the OMNI station to smoothly make the transition when flying over the station. Until then, the pilot when flying to an OMNI station would have to disengage the autopilot as the aircraft neared the station and then re-engage the autopilot to fly away from the OMNI station.

The area above the OMNI station was known as the "zone of confusion," and it grew bigger as altitude increased. When in this zone, the OMNI receiver would not have enough information to determine which direction to fly and would send irregular signals to the autopilot causing it to fly erratically, even dangerously.

Sperry had flight tested this improvement and had sent out kits to the Sperry autopilot users who were interested in this improvement. After I left Sperry and went to work for TI, I was making frequent trips from Dallas to New York.

On one of these flights I was traveling on a Braniff Douglas DC-6 that was equipped with a Sperry autopilot. I asked the stewardess to ask the captain if I could visit the cockpit and discuss the autopilot performance. She talked to the captain and he invited me up.

The captain had the autopilot on and it was engaged and coupled to an OMNI signal. As we approached an OMNI station, I asked the pilot if Braniff had installed the kit that allowed the aircraft to fly on autopilot over the OMNI Station without disengaging the signal. He said they had, offering to show me. We were almost directly above the OMNI station when the aircraft sharply banked right and then just as sharply banked left. The captain quickly switched to manual control. Apparently the cone of silence kit had not been installed in this system or the kit had malfunctioned.

When I returned to the cabin, the passengers were all wide-eyed, and the stewardesses were cleaning up some food and drinks that had gotten scattered. After this, I choose not to ask the captains if I could visit the cockpit.

SYNERGISM OF EXPERTISE

My new Sperry assignment in Dallas was very flexible in terms of when I needed to perform the functions of the job. I had started work on a Master's Degree in Electrical Engineering (MSEE) while in Tulsa. With a flexible working schedule, I resumed my studies at Southern Methodist University. I was awarded an MSEE at SMU on May 31, 1959. Math had always been easy for me and when we got to the information theory level classes, many in the class had difficulty.

There were three management level Texas Instruments (TI) staffers in several of my classes. They included a vice President in the military products division, a radar department manager, and a radar branch manager. We became friends and after class would go to the Egyptian Lounge on Mockingbird Lane for pizza. They would talk about how hard the homework was. I had more available time than they did to work on the homework, so when they asked me for help I gladly gave it.

Mel Barney

UNIVERSITY OF MICHIGAN COHERENT SIDE LOOKING RADAR (CSLR) RADAR PROGRAM

In the summer of 1958 Ray McCord asked me to come to work at TI in his radar department and I agreed. I had experience in automatic flight control systems and TI had just won a big contract with the University of Michigan to build a Coherent Side Looking Radar (CSLR). The mission of the CSLR was to give the United States military the ability to fly in a neutral area adjacent to the Soviet border and spy using the side looking radar. My experience in designing automatic pilots was a basic requirement in executing the University of Michigan Contract.

During my first day at work at TI, Ray called me into his office and told me that I was now the world's foremost expert on Doppler Inertial Navigation Systems (DINS) at TI. He instructed me to prepare a presentation on DINS, to be given to all of the engineers in the apparatus division (military products) in one month.

A DINS is a system that includes a Doppler Navigation System (DNS) and a Schuler Tuned Inertial Platform (STIP). This system produces a very accurate long range navigation system and short range stability and navigation accuracy. I was assigned to be the program manager of the DINS System and the flight test program.

TI had contracts with Kearfott Instruments (KI) in New Jersey and General Precision Laboratories (GPL) Systems in New York. KI produced the Shuler tuned inertial platform and GPL produced the Doppler radar system. My job was to coordinate the development and coupling of these two systems, so that they would provide the side looking radar with very precise measurements of the aircrafts deviations from an absolute straight flight path. I was also responsible for the flight test and development program

I spent about two days every other week in New York and New Jersey working with KI and GPL on the systems. Many times I would take a night course at SMU and catch a late flight to New York to visit GPL and KI. I would do my homework while on the trip and be ready for the next class when I returned.

The United States Army provided TI with four L-23s (Army version of the Beechcraft 'twin Bonanza) to receive the installation of the (CSLR) Systems. TI built a radome that looked like a bathtub and was about 14 feet long. The CSLR antenna was located under the L-23 inside of the radome.

The L-23 with bathtub radome in place

We had to point the antenna very accurately to get good results. For this, the mechanical engineers chose to use a hydraulic control system. On our first flight we had a severe problem. When the flight test engineer first turned the

CSLR System on the L-23 shook violently around the vertical axis. The mechanical engineers solved the problem by putting in small orifices to limit the rate of flow hydraulic fluid to the hydraulic actuators. With the antenna fixed, we started testing the CSLR. We would fly a flight, record the data, land, and examine the results.

FIRE IN THE COCKPIT

When the test aircraft was performing a test flight we maintained radio contact with the test engineer on the flight. Our call letter name was kinfolks.

On one of the early flight tests, Joe Mink, an excellent engineer, served as flight test engineer. Joe was an easy going very large affable guy with a slow southern drawl.

Just as the test run got going, Joe came on the radio and announced in a matter-of -fact tone, "Kinfolks, we have a fire in the cockpit."

"Where is it," I asked.

"It is on the side of my pants," Joe said, grabbing the airplane extinguisher to douse the fire.

They immediately landed and we found that the fire had been caused by a wire that had been crimped by the seat that Joe was sitting in.

As we continued on the flight test, we determined that the system did produce excellent maps of the area out to 100 miles to the side of the aircraft. However, the performance degraded rapidly when the aircraft was flying through turbulence. The system was able to identify a military tank at a range of 20 miles, provided the weather was relatively smooth.

BREAKTHROUGH TECHNOLOGY

During the 1960s and 1970s Texas Instruments (TI) built an impressive business in the high technology, highly classified military weapons development and production business. Much of this business was not visible to the general public and in many cases to the workers at TI. Two of the areas that I am familiar with were the radar and infrared programs. I will discuss several of these programs that are no longer militarily classified.

By the 1960's semiconductors had replaced vacuum tubes as the main components of most electronic systems. Jack Kilby, a friend of mine, invented the integrated circuit, which allowed transistors and other electronic components to be placed on a silicon wafer. I made several trips to Dayton, Ohio with Jack to encourage the engineers at Wright Patterson Air Force Base to include these devices in their new weapon systems. TI was a leader in adapting these integrated circuits in electronic systems.

One of TI's leadership positions was in the infrared sensor (night vision) systems. These included systems located beneath the aircraft that record the hot or warm areas that the aircraft flew near. One was the aircraft Forward Looking Infra-Red (FLIR) system that pointed forward in an aircraft giving the pilot a vision of warm or hot areas ahead. Another was the infrared sensor that guided the laser guided bombs to a laser spot on the ground.

INFRA-RED LINE SCANNER (IRLS)

This system included an infra-red (IR) sensor that was located beneath the aircraft and rotated rapidly. As the aircraft flew over, the IR detector found hot spots on the ground. The sensor output would be recorded on a continuously moving film recording where the hot spots, such as people, vehicles, or fires, were located. This information could then be used to plan attacks or destroy the targets. It proved to be a useful military tool.

One sad anecdote was an event that one of the engineers on the IRLS program told me about. The Tennessee alcoholic tax program was trying to find and destroy illegal liquor stills throughout the state. They reasoned that they could use the IRLS to find out where the liquor stills were located. They used the Aero Commander aircraft with the IRLS installed to locate the stills. The system worked well and there were many stills located and destroyed. However, the illegal still operators finally figured out how they were being located. They armed themselves and were able to shoot down the Aero Commander, killing the entire crew.

ELEPHANTS

In my opinion, the most brilliant marketing engineer at TI at that time was Mickey McCray. He was responsible for selling the Forward Looking Infrared (FLIR) system to our military customers. In the early stages, many were skeptical about FLIR Systems. Mickey set up a demonstration in the tower of the North Building at the TI Central Expressway Site. He invited a group of military people from all of the branches of the armed services to observe the performance. On the night of the demonstration he had the FLIR pointed toward the TI parking lot and a field on the other side of the lot. The FLIR worked well and the observers could see the people and cars moving in the lot.

All of a sudden the FLIR showed three elephants walking single file across the field. The observers first thought it was a hoax. Then Mickey took them out to the field to see that they were real elephants. Mickey had met with an elephant trainer in a circus that was in Dallas at that time. He paid the trainer to bring three elephants to TI on the appointed date and time, and parade across the field.

WELDON WORD: FATHER OF THE LASER GUIDED BOMB

One of my good friends at TI was Weldon Word. Weldon had an idea about using a laser beam and infrared sensors to guide a bomb to a specific target. The idea was to have a highly stabilized laser beam from an aircraft or from the ground pointed at a specific target, then use infrared sensors on the bomb to guide itself to that laser spot. The sensor on the bomb was not a complicated device. It had four infrared detector surfaces. By setting up the circuitry to use the opposing sensor output magnitudes to find the position where they were of equal magnitude, the sensors could be made to point directly at the laser spot. Once Weldon demonstrated the system at the Naval Ordinance Test Station (NOTS) at China Lake, California, TI was in the laser guided bomb business.

THE NEXT TI ASSIGNMENT

The University of Michigan project was completed in a couple of years. On May 1, 1960, Gary Powers, a CIA U-2 pilot was shot down by the Russians while flying at a very high altitude. This caused great concern in the United States military community. Their primary plan had been to monitor Russia's H Bomb development and, if necessary, attack the Soviets from a very high altitude.

Radar beams travel in straight lines. The curvature of the earth will prevent radars use in detecting very low flying aircraft until they are too close to shoot down. With this in mind the Air Force, Navy, and Marine Corps started looking for some way to penetrate Russian airspace without being detected. They all started to think the best way to execute an attack would be at very low altitude.

The competition between the Soviet Union and the United States to gain a technology advantage for delivering H-bombs to destroy the other had become a major military priority. TI had been developing a drone mono-pulse radar that would provide vertical guidance for an unmanned drone. Having gained substantial expertise in the design of automatic pilots at Sperry, I reasoned that TI could develop an Automatic Terrain Following Radar (ATFR) System that would fly a manned aircraft safely at an altitude of 200 feet with the pilot's hands off of the controls.

I approached Ray McCord, suggesting that TI provide me with the funds to develop an ATFR System. After detailed technical discussions with other engineers with pertinent expertise, Ray asked for $100,000 to fund the program. The project was ready to start and I was asked to present the development plan for the system to the annual TI project review meeting.

The presentation went well and I thought I had the program sold, when Senior Vice President Wally Joyce interrupted and said that the project was too dangerous and could expose TI to huge liability lawsuits if the aircraft crashed. Pat Haggerty, then President of TI, studied the development plan and overruled Wally Joyce. TI was to proceed with the program and with funding. The program was militarily classified as secret. TI selected me to be the program manager.

THE AUTOMATIC TERRAIN FOLLOWING RADAR SYSTEM (ATFRS) DEVELOPMENT AND FLIGHT TEST PROGRAM

TI leased a used Douglas B-26 from Joe Truhill. I bought a used Sperry A-12 Autopilot, and had it installed in the B-26 and certified by the FAA. We then started the development and testing of the system. We had a recording radar altimeter so that we could record the altitude performance of the system during the flight tests. We had a planned course with known terrain elevations along the flight test path. This allowed us to compare the deviation from the ideal flight path along the flight test course.

We had an excellent team of engineers and technicians including Hal Tichnor, Bill Walton, and eight others. Hal, Bill, and I flew all of the test and demonstration flights. When we flew development flights, Joe Truhill would pilot the aircraft and monitor the test flight altitude. Joe would manually takeover from the ATFR System if the aircraft appeared to be flying into the ground. There were more than a dozen occasions early in the program where Joe had to take over. One engineer sat in the copilot's seat and operated the ATFR System. He would also perform the function of a backup safety monitor. The third crew member tweaked the system as needed and monitored the recording instruments.

I have the flight test logs from all of these flights. A copy of these flight logs may be found in the appendix. From this flight log, I counted 153 military and civilian people who participated in these demonstrations flights. Besides the local Dallas area, flight demonstrations were flown out of Dayton, Ohio, Atlanta, Georgia, Washington, D. C., and over Rich Mountain in eastern Oklahoma.

We flew 55 flights before we were confident enough to

take observers. Subsequently a total of 226 development, test, and demonstration flights were flown. The demonstration flights included military and civilian observers from the U. S., and British, Army, Navy, Marine, Air Force, civil service engineers, and engineers from other aerospace companies. The usual crew included Hal Tichnor, Bill Walton, or me. These flights were dangerous. Flying over mountainous terrain at 200 foot altitude, was both thrilling and frightening. Loss of an engine or equipment malfunction could cause the B-26 to crash very quickly.

DEVELOPMENT, TEST AND DEMONSTRATION OF THE ATFRS

On our earliest test flights we ran into severe problems. The earliest problem was setting the coupling dynamics of the aircraft, the autopilot, and the radar so that a smooth transition would be made when flying over level or rough terrain. The first time we switched the ATFR System on, the aircraft went into an almost violent roller coaster maneuver. After studying these gyrations on our computer, we were able to tweak the dynamics to eliminate this problem.

There were several different phases in the flight tests that we flew. The first was to demonstrate to the Federal Aviation Agency (FAA) that the installation and operation of the autopilot and radar did not cause flight hazards to the aircraft. Next was to solve specific problems. These flights were flown mostly in Dallas. Flights to evaluate and record the system performance were done over the mountains in Eastern Oklahoma. The last phase was to demonstrate the system performance for potential customers. These flights were dangerous and in many cases the potential customers did not want to participate in a second flight.

One of the earliest and most serious problems occurred

when going up the side of a mountain. The aircraft would get almost to the top of the mountain and suddenly dive at the peak. We soon realized that the problem was with the Transmit Receive Tube (TRT). We went to the supplier and asked him to develop a TRT that would protect the receiver but allow the return radar transmitted signal to enter the receiver at 700 feet. The vender was able to do so after a few weeks of development time.

Another problem was with tall towers. If the radar was pointed directly at the tower, it would provide the necessary up signal to clear tower. However, if it was pointed slightly off of the tower, it would not see the supporting cables that held the tower up. We solved this problem by having a cross scan that would direct the radar up, down and latterly across the flight path.

For our primary evaluation route, we picked a route that took us to Rich Mountain in east central Oklahoma. We picked it because it had an OMNI navigation beacon on the tallest mountain. We also knew the precise terrain elevation of our flight path. After each flight we would compare the recorded altitude above the ground during the test flight with previous test flights. We then modified the equipment dynamics in a manner that optimized the flight performance.

During the period that I was involved in the Automatic Terrain Following Radar Programs (ATFR), I was issued three patents that improved the system performance. These patents were instrumental in the success of the system programs. The description of all six of my patents may be found in the appendix.

After we had flown more than 120 flights and were getting good results, Dr. Frank Pelton, head of the Cornell Aeronautical Laboratories, contacted me to see if he could come to Dallas and fly on one of our developmental flights.

He was developing a similar non-automatic system for the Navy A-6 Aircraft. He came to Dallas and flew a test flight with us. He was impressed. We agreed to stay in contact on the progress with our separate programs. He asked me to be a panel member at the Low Level Penetration Symposium at the Paris Air Show. I accepted. Our program was the only program discussed that had actually flown a system that automatically flew the aircraft when coupled to the autopilot.

ENTER THE CIA

Shortly after the Pelton visit, I was told to go to Washington D. C. and check into the Mayflower Hotel after which I would be contacted. A couple of hours after I had checked in to the Hotel, I got a call from a man in the lobby who wanted to come talk to me. He came up to my room and identified himself as the chief engineer for the Montana Forest Service. I had enough military security experience to realize that he was from the CIA. He asked if I could deliver an ATFR System to an as yet unidentified location, then asked how long it would take and how much it would cost. I told him it would cost $200,000 and would take about nine months. I asked about a contract and security coverage for this classified system. He said that I did not have to worry about contracts or security clearances, as he would set up the payment process directly with the TI "bean counters" and the security details with the TI Security Department.

By the time I returned to Dallas, the contracts department had all of the information they needed to fund the program. The TI Security Department also had the needed clearances prepared. We built a second system similar to the one we were testing. When we finished we were told to deliver it to the Naval Ordinance Test Station (NOTS) at China Lake, California.

Over the next six months they installed it in a Navy A-6 aircraft. I made several trips to NOTS to assist. When the installation was finished I was invited to go to NOTS and fly in the A-6 on a test flight. The flight performance of the ATFR System was as advertised.

APPALACHIAN MOUNTAINS

After we had proven the system performed as expected, other TI Managers began asking to participate in test flights. One of these was Grant Dove, the Manager of the Washington Office. After participating in a test flight, Grant asked if we could demonstrate the system to high level pentagon officials in Washington. I said yes and we prepared to spend two weeks in D.C. demonstrating the system over the Appalachian Mountains. I told Grant we needed special security arrangements to guard the aircraft while in Washington because it had classified equipment on board. Grant arranged the necessary security to guard the B-26 when not in use.

During the two weeks we demonstrated the system to approximately 35 military people with ranks from admiral, general, through lieutenant and ensign. The system functioned perfectly. Most of the guest passengers were very impressed. Some were truly frightened.

NEAR DISASTROUS FLIGHT

After the last scheduled flight, it was my turn to fly with Joe and the two guest observers. We flew the course auto-

matically and the system topped the mountains at an altitude of close to 200 feet. Joe had climbed to 1,000 feet and
I was feeling good about the systems performance during
the two weeks. We suddenly heard an explosion as the B-26
veered to the left. We looked out and saw the left engine on
fire. We could see a hole where a cylinder had apparently
been blown through the engine's outer covering.

Joe managed to feather the propeller of the left engine
to reduce air resistance. He declared Mayday on the radio
and asked for guidance and assistance during the 50 mile
flight back to National Airport. National Airport Controllers never acknowledged his Mayday call. We limped back
to the airport at an altitude of 1000 feet, which used all the
power Joe could coax out of the right engine.

Joe approached the airport and lined up on runway 120.
We then heard the tower demanding that the unidentified
aircraft approaching runway 120 go around. Joe flew on
around and lined up with runway 150. Again the tower
controller commanded us to go around. Joe decided to land
on runway 150 anyway. As we safely touched the ground on
runway 150 the tower controller finally gave us permission
to land on runway 150. Commercial aircraft in the area
had heard Joe's distress call and were able to tell the controllers in the tower that we had a real problem. By the
time Joe stopped the airplane, we were surrounded by fire
trucks and emergency equipment. Hal, Bill and I flew back
to Dallas on Braniff Airlines. Joe had the engine repaired,
and two weeks later I returned to Washington and flew
back to Dallas with Joe.

During the decade of the 1960's TI gained a reputation
as the only company to implement an automatic terrain
following radar and demonstrate safe automatic flight at
200 ft altitude. These credentials along with other TI technical capabilities allowed TI to bid on and win more than

one hundred million dollars worth of forward looking radar contracts. These contracts included forward looking radars for the RF4-C, F-111, C-130, A-6 aircraft, and, many other aircraft.

After demonstrating the feasibility of automatic flight at 200 foot altitude in Washington, there was much interest from all of the military services. They were interested in this new capability. The interest came from users of helicopters, cargo and troop carriers, and CIA missions.

HELICOPTERS: CAREFUL WHAT YOU ASK FOR!

I have never been a fan of helicopters. The structure of the rotor blades is not strong enough to support the aircraft by themselves. The centrifugal force of the rotating blades adds extra strength to support the weight of the helicopter. Also, their forward velocity is limited. During my career I experienced several flights on helicopters. I did not feel comfortable on any of them. Some of these flights are discussed below.

Bell Helicopter was talking to TI about radar for one of their new military helicopters. They invited TI to send an engineer to their Dallas plant. I was chosen and we discussed the specifications that they needed to achieve their military requirements. After the meeting, the engineers offered me a flight demonstration on one of the helicopters. Feeling I needed the experience, I accepted and they took me out to their flight test area. I boarded with the pilot and a Bell engineer and sat in the right seat. We took off and went through a series of routine maneuvers. It was interesting and fun till I made the mistake of asking what would happen if we lost an engine. The pilot immediately offered to demonstrate.

He pulled the throttle all of the way back and the helicopter dropped like a rock. My stomach was in my throat. He then used the collective control to change the angle of the rotor blades to a pitch that would cause the blades to spin faster as the upward air flowed over the blades. This caused the rotor blades to spin rapidly. He gradually moved the throttle forward and we were back in a normal flight mode. If he had really had a power loss, he would have allowed the helicopter to continue dropping. Just before he reached the ground he would use the momentum in the rapidly rotating rotor blades and the rotor pitch control to make a "soft landing."

MARINE INTEREST IN TERRAIN FOLLOWING RADAR FOR THEIR HELICOPTER MISSIONS

I was invited to visit the Marines in San Diego to discuss the capabilities of the ATFR System and its potential for controlling a helicopter at low altitude. It became apparent that controlling a helicopter with an ATFR System was a whole new world. It would require a big research program to develop a system that could safely and satisfactorily fly their missions.

They took me on a simulated mission in the San Diego area. I have to say that flying the helicopter at low level induced much more angst in me than flying the TI B-26 at low level. TI did not pursue the Marine low level ATFR System business.

THE FIRST BIG TI
FORWARD LOOKING RADAR CONTRACT

With the success of the Automatic Terrain Radar we developed and demonstrated for all branches of the United States military, TI was in a highly competitive position to compete with the other military airborne forward looking radar manufacturers, such as Westinghouse, Raytheon, Norden, and, Autonetics.

The first big competition we won was for the radar for the McConnell RF-4C. I was responsible for writing the proposal section that included the automatic terrain following function. I proposed a modified version of the radar we had been demonstrating over the preceding year. After the first prototype system was delivered, Sandy McDonnell, Chairman of the Board at McDonnell, called the TI top managers to St. Louis and told them the APQ-99 would not perform satisfactorily in the RF-4C, as the forward looking mapping function was inadequate. McDonnell threatened to cancel the program.

TI looked for and found an extremely smart engineering manager in Houston who had impressed management with his ability to solve tough engineering problems. The manager was moved to Dallas and given charge of the APQ-99 program and access to all TI resources. I was picked to solve problems relating to the terrain following radar.

I examined the flight results and realized that the lower side lobes resulting from the parabolic vertical beam antenna were causing false fly up commands and poor mapping performance. These false commands interrupted the smooth elevation flight of the aircraft. I asked the manager of TI's antenna design laboratory to build a 24 inch parabolic horizontal shape and a cosecant-squared elevation shape antenna. Technicians installed this new antenna on an APG-99 radar system.

I rented a room on the top of the Braniff Building, 200 feet above the ground. At this height the radar could look out the window and operate like an RF-4C flying at 200 foot altitude. We could make changes to the system to eliminate problems while the radar was operating. It was a perfect site to prove the capability of the APQ-99 with the new antenna. After several design changes in the elevation mono-pulse receiver and addition of the new antenna, the lower side lobe problem was gone. The antenna design for the APQ-99 was changed to the new design.

ATTACK RADAR SYSTEMS BRANCH

During the mid-1960s, TI's capability to automatically fly at a 200 foot altitude played a key role in their winning several large airborne radar contracts. For TI's bid on the forward-looking radar for the LTV A-7 aircraft, I was the proposal manager. Dean Thomas of LTV and I spent weeks in negotiating the detailed specifications for the radar and the prices for any changes.

The most unusual contractual inclusions were that LTV would impose a $1000 penalty for each ounce that each radar weighed over 200 pounds and that they would impose a $1000 penalty for each day that each radar was delivered after the contracted date.

TI won the contract and I was pleased to be the program manager. Our division vice-president told me that TI had better not have to pay either of these fines for being overweight or late in delivery. Every time LTV wanted to change any part of the specification, beside the increase in the contract price, I would insist on extra ounces or delivery schedule relief. Fortunately, we were able to deliver the radars on time, and they weighed slightly less than 200 pounds. It is ironic that by the time the A-7 was delivered, they had to add ballast in the nose, in order to meet the weight and balance specifications for the aircraft.

After the radar was in production and installed in the A-7 aircraft, The Navy invited me to see the system operate on the USS Ranger Aircraft Carrier off the coast of California. It was a thrill taking off and landing on the big carrier. I spent a week observing the system performance in the A-7s flying off of the aircraft carrier. I discussed the system performance with the pilots and answered their questions. At night I would go to the flight operations tower and see the aircraft land and take off. I believe that the Navy pilots who qualify for that assignment are the most skilled and brave military people in the world. To watch those pilots land and take off from a pitching aircraft carrier deck at night in marginal weather was impressive.

AIRPORT SURVEILLANCE RADARS

My next TI assignment was to manage the Airport surveillance Radar Department. This department had sold airport surveillance radars to more than 150 large airports in the United States and the rest of the world.

During the late 1950s and 1960s the United States had many aid programs for developing countries which included money to purchase airport surveillance radars. Good, safe airports were essential for these countries to pursue their economic initiatives. TI kept in close contact with those countries using TI radars to make sure that the radars were functioning properly, and that they maintained an adequate supply of parts.

During this period the United States Federal Aviation

Agency was purchasing the next generation of Airport Radar Terminal Systems (ARTS-3). The ARTS-3 was an improvement over previous systems, in that it used the latest computer techniques to assist the air traffic controller in his job. TI made a proposal to provide this equipment and won the contract.

While managing this department I gained a lot of experience with the international market, which Texas Instruments was interested in focusing more on. I traded information with the Dallas CIA agent relative to the political and economic situations of the countries who were potential customers.

INTERNATIONAL MARKETING

My department was performing satisfactorily and we had a substantial backlog of business. I was then asked to take over the position of Director of International Marketing for Texas Instruments. In this new job I became more exposed to the Cold War and information exchange with the CIA.

My travels in many countries made me realize that people around the world are not so different. People generally treat you in the same manner which you treat them. The religions I observed usually observed the equivalent of both the Ten Commandments and the golden rule.

HOW U. S. WON COLD WAR

During and after World War II, the United States had three of the best Presidents of all time. Presidents Roosevelt, Truman, and Eisenhower had the foresight to prepare not only the United States, but a larger part of the non-communist nations for the battle to come against the communist nations.

Roosevelt created the G. I. Bill of Rights, Truman the Marshall Plan, and Eisenhower the Interstate Highway System. The Marshall plan played a big role in restoring the destroyed European countries' economies. These economies became markets for the new products developed by the Americans.

THE G. I. BILL OF RIGHTS

After World War II, about ten million soldiers returned home. They were a mature and serious group of men and women. They had experienced the Great Depression. Most of their parents had not attended college, but, had stressed to them that a college education was important to their future success. President Harry Truman, who had fought in World War I, also knew the importance of a college education. He was a key proponent of the G. I. Bill of Rights initiated by his predecessor Franklin Roosevelt.

This bill provided returning soldiers a chance to go to college at the expense of the United States Government. The returning veterans had learned a lot about technology and its importance in a competitive society. Many veterans pursued engineering and scientific degrees. The resulting supply of engineers, and scientists, far outnumbered the numbers in other countries. Their skills were the basis of the unparalleled economic success of the United States over the next forty years.

The engineering and scientific professions are self proliferating. The more they created, invented, and innovated, the more there was to create, invent, and innovate.

The United States produced far more technically educated people than did Russia for two main reasons. One was that war casualties of young Russians, was almost ten times that of the U. S. Almost a whole generation (mostly men) was lost in the war. The other was that the Russians did not have an education program equal to the G. I Bill of Rights.

Eisenhower, a rare general who hated war, developed the national programs that would use the talents of the newly educated engineers and scientists. One of these was the Interstate Highway System (IHS) that stimulated the automobile, tourist, construction, and other industries. These actions, along with other farsighted programs, propelled the United States into forty years of world economic and technological leadership.

In the long back-and-forth battle between communism and capitalism, a major objective was to deliver the H-bomb on the enemy. The United States was spying on the Soviet Union with the extremely high altitude U-2 spy planes. The Soviet countermeasure was to develop a missile that could reach high enough to shoot down the U-2. When Gary Powers was shot down on May 1, 1960, the United States military community realized they could not threaten to strike from high altitudes.

The countermeasure was covert penetration of enemy airspace at low altitude, which all but eliminated the enemy's ability to detect the aircraft until it was too late to shoot it down. The curvature of the earth prevents the radar detection of the attacking aircraft until it is very close to the radar site. Flying high-speed aircraft at this altitude was almost impossible to accomplish against a target located over hundreds of miles of enemy territory. For this task, the aircraft must be flown automatically at low altitude. This logic led our military to fund development of the

Automatic Terrain Following Radar (ATFR) System.

Each time the one side was forced to develop the next countermeasure to defeat a countermeasure that had been put in service, the price of development and production escalated. Both Americans and Soviets were being forced to spend more and more on these measures. National spending on military products reduces the amount of funding countries can spend on their own needs and infrastructure. Ultimately, the country that could win the counter measures battle while keeping its citizens from revolting would win the Cold War.

MARKETING IN A CONTENTIOUS ENVIRONMENT

During my first incursion behind the Iron Curtain in September of 1972, I could only get communist television channels in my Intourist Hotel room. However, by my second incursion in 1973, the same hotel had added the British Broadcast Company (BBC) Station to their channel offerings. Upon my return, I told my wife that the United States would soon win the Cold War because the Soviet citizens could now see how far their lifestyles lagged behind those found in non-communist countries. This was the point in time when Nixon and Brezhnev began to talk about Détente.

BLACK PROGRAMS

Black programs played a big part in the counter measures contest. Most of my professional career as an electrical engineer was spent inventing, developing, and marketing weapons of war. During a long period of my career, I had the highest security clearances. The levels of security clearances issued during my career were Strictly Private, Confidential, Secret, Top Secret, and Black. Black programs were only known about by a few congressmen, the CIA, the president, and the company responsible for the program. Very little paperwork was involved and any paperwork was camouflaged. The work done on the program was hidden both electronically and visually from other areas.

I have already discussed the first black program that I participated in after meeting with a CIA agent in the Mayflower hotel in Washington D. C. This first visit led to my association with the Dallas CIA agent that lasted more than twenty years. He provided me with the current CIA Factbooks on the countries I planned to visit and advised me of what dangers or other obstacles to expect. In many countries the corruption was so bad that it was not worthwhile spending travel dollars to visit.

IRON CURTAIN INCURSIONS

The Cold War, which was primarily between the Soviet Union and the United States, was at its peak in the early 1970s. The Iron Curtain, or barrier along the border between the countries of Eastern and Western Europe, was difficult to penetrate. President Nixon and Premier Brezhnev were trying to lower the level of angst between their two countries with their détente initiative.

In 1972 Russia would not issue visas to American citizens. However, in addition to Moscow, my travels included trips to Leipzig, Belgrade, and Budapest. One of these visits included a trip to an electronics technology fair in Leipzig, East Germany. These visits supported the objective of an improvement in the exchange of communications between communist and capitalist nations.

My first visit to Moscow in October of 1972 was a real adventure. I had concerns about my personal safety and questioned what results that my visit could achieve. I went through an interesting process to be able to make this visit.

It all started with the forming of a coalition between IBM, Westinghouse, Raytheon and TI in order to bid on a new Soviet Civil Aviation Control System. In July of 1973, more than 50 upper level managers and engineers from these four companies met in Moscow to participate in the "USSR/US Aeronautical Technology Symposium and Exhibit" (U/UATSE). As a result of this visit, nine top level Russian officials were invited to visit each of the four coalition companies in December of 1972.

WHY I WANTED TO VISIT MOSCOW

By the summer of 1972, I had visited more than 30 countries as the Director of International Marketing for Texas Instruments. In my new assignment, my association with the CIA continued. I heard through my CIA contact, that the Soviets were planning to upgrade their civil aviation infrastructure. I was given the name of Tatiana Anodina, Ph.D., as a possible contact in Moscow. Dr. Anodina was the Director of Aeronautical Tecnology Research (DATR) for the USSR. (Although this was early in her career, you can "google" her name today to find that she is still a high-level Russian avaiation official.)

TI had a marketing representative, Dr. Neils Jasper, in Bonn, Germany. I asked him to try and set up a visit for me with Dr. Anodina. He said I could not get an American visa for the Soviet Union, but could possibly get one through a neutral European Country. I asked Neils to see if he could contact Dr. Anodina. He made the contact with her. She was interested and suggested that I go to Sweden and request the visa to visit Moscow from there.

On September 26, 1972, I traveled to Teheran, Iran. While there, I visited the seismic listening station nearby that TI had been hired by our government to set up to listen for the detonation of H-bombs in Russia. By looking at the seismic sensor recordings from a multiple of delicate instruments, strategically located around the explosion site, the petroleum engineers could accurately predict areas where there were oil sands. The seismic sensors in Iran were listening for vibrations from Soviet H-bomb tests.

The next day, Dr. Seitz, a member of the TI Board of Directors treated Richard and me to a trip to the "Iranian Riviera" on the Caspian Sea. The following morning, I flew from Teheran to Stockholm Sweden on Aeroflot, the major Soviet airline. I have to admit I had a moderate level of angst. Most of the passengers spoke only Russian.

In Stockholm, I went to the Russian Embassy and requested a visa to visit Moscow. I was told to check back every day to see if a Visa had been approved. With nothing else to do, I visited the Swedish Aviation Agency and, in discussions with engineers, learned that they planned to bid on an upcoming air traffic control system for the Soviet Civil Aviation Agency. I also went to a Swedish opera and enjoyed other Stockholm tourist attractions. After seven days the Russian embassy had received permission to issue my visa.

Before leaving Dallas, I had been briefed by my CIA contact on the dos and don'ts of visiting Russia during the cold war. Among other things, he mentioned that valuables such as gold, rings, jewelry, or other items not readily available to the Soviets should not be exchanged. He asked me to remember all the information I could about who the most influential government officials were.

Upon arrival in Moscow, I took a taxi to the Intourist Hotel, where it was prearranged that I would meet up with Neils Jasper. After checking in, I located Neils in the hotel dining room. We sat at a table for four. Just as we noticed that the staff was filling tables with people who had not come together, two Russians sat down at our table. In broken English, they started a friendly conversation. During our chat, one of them looked at my college graduation ring and commented that it was very beautiful. He asked if I would be willing to sell it for 500 dollars; a sum far above its value. Fortunately, I remembered the advice from my CIA friend and declined. We had a fine meal and retired to our rooms.

The next morning, we headed to the meeting which Neils had previously set up with the CAO. She was a beautiful blonde lady who looked to be in her mid-thirties. At the meeting, we were seated at a large conference table. Each attendee had an empty glass for the water pitchers spaced down the table. Everyone, including Neils and me, filled their glasses. Thirsty, I took a drink and was startled to discover that what I assumed was water was actually straight vodka. I then asked for and received water.

My presentation included descriptions of civil aviation products that TI had produced for many other countries. I then asked if they were planning to update their civil aviation infrastructure, and if so, if they would allow American firms to compete for this system. The CAO said that they were looking for the best system regardless of who supplied it.

We then had a technical session during which the Russians asked questions about TI's civil aviation equipment. I answered their questions. Since the TI equipment had been in service all over the world, including some Soviet allies, there was little chance of giving them information that might have military value. We arranged for me to make direct contact with the CAO and adjourned the meeting. I then returned to Dallas.

FORMING THE U.S. TEAM

After returning from Moscow, I contacted my counter parts at IBM, Westinghouse, and Raytheon. At that time within the Federal Aviation Administration (FAA), IBM provided the central computing system for the air traffic control system, Westinghouse supplied the long range regional radar systems, Raytheon supplied the airport radar terminal display systems, and TI supplied the terminal radar systems in all American airports as well as those in many other countries. All agreed to participate and we met in Washington D. C. in late October of 1972 to plan the proposal for the Soviet air traffic control program.

IBM was unanimously chosen to be the proposal manager for the bid. I was designated as the information focal point between our team of companies, the CIA, and the Soviets. I briefed my CIA contact and he encouraged us to proceed with the proposal.

I met with and updated my CIA contact and then contacted the Russian CAO. She expressed pleasure with the excellent quartet of companies participating in the bid. She then asked whether I could arrange for her and her team of nine experts to visit each company. My CIA contact agreed to help me get the necessary approvals for the visit. He insisted on a CIA presence at every meeting with the Soviet team during the entire visit and all parties agreed.

I called my contact to advise her that the visit was a go and suggested times for her team to visit each of the four companies. The visit to TI was scheduled for early December of 1972.

The Soviets appreciated our work on this initiative. During their visit their CAO presented me with two gifts of appreciation for my role in the venture. One was an album of classical Russian music by famous Russian composers. The second gift was a beautiful brooch similar to those I had seen in the Armory Museum in Moscow.

Russian music album featuring the voice of Chaliapin in classics such as Rimski-Korsakov's "Fortune Teller".

Mel Barney

Russian Brooch received as a gift.

SOVIET TEAM'S VISIT
TO TI IN DECEMBER, 1972

We met the Soviet visitors at Love Field Airport in Dallas. All of them spoke English reasonably well. We first took all nine team members to their hotel and gave them time to rest. By observing their actions and participation in technical discussions, we later surmised that three of them were KGB Agents. We had set up two days of meetings that included hardware demonstrations and discussions about technical specifications for the TI Radars to be included in our proposal. The meetings were attended by several TI vice presidents and high level managers, as well as our best radar engineers.

The Soviet visitors were very interested in American culture, so we took them out to some of the finest restaurants in Dallas for long lunches. We showed them our most interesting local attractions. At their request we took them to Dealey Plaza, where President Kennedy was shot. We traveled in four different cars, which allowed us to answer their questions. As it turned out they were completely amazed by the TI parking lots with all of the workers' cars. They could hardly believe that the cars belonged to the workers. They were equally fascinated with the supermarkets, finding the quantity of products and low prices hard to believe. Low-cost stores like Target were another source of amazement for our guests.

I was driving the car with the CAO and her top engineer. After lunch she asked to go to a department store. They could not buy blue jeans in Moscow. She wanted to buy eight or ten pair for her son and some of her relatives. I took them to North Park mall and Neiman Marcus. She bought blue jeans and several other items not available in Moscow. When I had been in Russia earlier, I was taken to Moscow's equivalent to Neiman Marcus; a store called GUM. That store had many products, but they were much more expensive than the equivalent products here.

The North Park stop made us late returning to TI for the afternoon meeting and two Soviets were extremely agitated by our tardiness. Later, we assumed that those two were the KGB Agents and their job was to see that the other members of the group did not escape and claim asylum as many prominent Russians had already done by then. We finished our meetings, taking our guests to Love Field the next morning to continue on to tour the other three companies.

During the next five months, representatives for all four companies worked to draft our proposal for the Soviet air traffic control system contract. The proposal was to be submitted at a symposium in Moscow in mid July of 1973. The Soviet CAO wanted to have an air traffic control technology exchange between American and Russian engineers. The attendees would include 10 to 15 engineers, managers, and corporate officers from each of the four American companies. She invited us all to bring our wives, promising that an appropriate entertainment agenda would be planned for them. She also suggested that the official name of the symposium be "USSR/US Aeronautical Technology Symposium and Exhibit" (U/UATSE).

I discussed the Russian visit and proposal for the U/UATSE with my CIA contact and the other three members of the proposal team. With all in agreement, the event was set for July 18 through July 25, 1973.

USSR/US AERONAUTICAL TECHNOLOGY SYMPOSIUM AND EXHIBIT

Officers, managers and engineers from IBM Westinghouse, Raytheon, and TI traveled to Moscow for the symposium, most with their wives. Each company had a booth displaying their equipment and related technology. The Russians also had exhibits. Panel discussion covered each related technology area. It was a custom in Russia to exchange lapel pins representing the company or part of the country the individual was from.

Lapel pins collected at Russian symposium

The Russians had set up lavish events for us, including The Bolshoi Ballet's performance of Swan Lake, a visit to the famous Russian Armory Museum, a shopping trip to GUM Department Store, and dinner at a famous Russian restaurant. We also attended a cocktail party sponsored by our Ambassador at the U.S. Embassy.

Moscow was very clean. We saw no litter or trash of any kind to mar the splendid landmarks. Compared to the London Underground, or the Paris Metro, the Moscow subway was more like a museum. It was such a well planned system, that we were able to take the subway to the U/UATSE site, our hotel, the theaters, and all other meetings and sight-seeing stops. It was fast and inexpensive and there were famous paintings and beautiful chandeliers everywhere.

The wives of participants were treated to many once-in-a-lifetime adventures including a two day visit to St. Petersburg on a splendid overnight train. In St. Petersburg, they visited the famous Hermitage Museum. During World War II the city was under siege and blockade for a period of 900 days. They also toured famous landmarks such as the monument to the tens of thousands of Russians who were killed by the Nazi Army during World War II.

During tours in Moscow, the ladies were treated to luncheons featuring Russian caviar, visits to Moscow churches (including St. Basil's Cathedral), and tours of the famous GUM Department Store and numerous other famous Russian landmarks. They saw a long line waiting to get into a department store. They asked about it, and were told that the people had government coupons to get boots.

THE RETURN TO DALLAS AND WAIT FOR THE RUSSIAN SYSTEM SELECTION

Several months after returning to Dallas we anxiously awaited the Russian selection of a vendor to build their new air traffic control system. As it turned out, a team including Sweden and France was awarded the contract. We were disappointed, but felt we had learned enough about the other competitors to have made the effort worthwhile. The CIA was satisfied with the information they'd gathered throughout the process.

LEIPZIP ELECTRONICS FAIR

TI had three technology areas interested in international business: the Geophysical Services Group, the Semiconductor Group, and the Equipment Group. Dr. Neils Jasper, our European marketing engineer, advised us of an upcoming Electronics Fair in Leipzig, East Germany. All three TI groups were interested in attending the Fair to see what the communist countries were developing.

We discussed a trip to this fair with my CIA contact in Dallas. He encouraged us to see if we could get visas to attend. Neils was able to get visas for himself and only three others. I was one of the three. We were instructed to go from West Germany to East Germany directly. We planned to rent a car and drive from Frankfort to Leipzig, which included eighty miles to the East German Border then another one hundred and twenty to Leipzig.

The two other attendees and I flew to Frankfort to meet Neils and we started our drive to the Leipzig Fair. When we got to the East German Border the guards acted surprised to see us. They examined our visas and passports, made several phone calls, but finally let us into East Germany. This delay made us worry about getting back out of East Germany.

At the Fair, we were surprised to find that we were technologically on par, and in some cases among the most advanced. The communist attendees had access to American technology through many neutral countries and through American technology-oriented magazines. After three or four days, we headed back to the border. We went through the same worrisome routine as before, but were eventually granted permission to pass into West Germany. We flew back from Frankfort to Dallas. The three of us set up an appointment with our Dallas CIA friend and were debriefed by him.

INTERNATIONAL ADVENTURES

As Director of International Marketing for TI during the 1970s, I experienced many interesting events in many parts of the world. These ranged from being kidnaped in Lagos, Nigeria to being honored in New Delhi, India with a Sunday afternoon croquet match by the TI Agent at his weekend retreat. This event was attended by the Ambassadors from South Korea and Malaysia.

My profound observation from all of these visits was that most people in all parts of the world are not that much different. They tend to treat you in a manner that you treat them. Of the many different religions I observed, I realized that most of them had, as a basic tenant, belief in the Golden Rule and some equivalent of the Ten Commandments.

My job included monitoring needs and finding business for TI all over the world. In this assignment I visited most of TI's worldwide facilities, and countries where TI had won contracts or was pursuing new contracts. Most of the time I traveled alone but on some trips I traveled with the corporate executives and engineers. On some of the trips I was able to take my wife, Carolyn.

My support group included several overseas marketing engineers, and many TI agents who received commissions when TI won contracts that they assisted with. I used many information sources to identify business opportunities. Some of them were the FAA, the CIA, the "Commerce Business Daily" publication, U.S. Aid Organization, TI's agents located in foreign countries, and military and commercial attachés in the U.S. Embassies.

KUALA LUMPUR: 272 STEPS TO THE BATU HINDU SHRINE.

TI had an integrated circuit factory in Kuala Lumpur which I was invited to visit to meet with the managers of the facility. Kuala Lumpur is a beautiful prosperous city in the middle of the Malaysian Jungle. My route to Kuala

Lumpur from the airport was a modern highway through miles of rubber trees that were a key source of rubber during World War II. One of the main attractions of the city was the Bantu Hindu Shrine. There were 272 wide steps up to the shrine. These had to be climbed in order to visit this beautiful Buddhist temple. Visitors were forbidden to disturb the monkeys, which were plentiful and aggressive. I learned the hard way that it was a mistake to climb the steps with food in your hands. The monkeys would eventually steal the food right out of your hands. Beside the shrine was a pewter shop. I bought some beautiful pieces of pewter to bring home to Carolyn.

Pewter purchased in Kuala Lumpur

Mel Barney

CHASED BY A LION
IN A NAIROBI NATIONAL PARK

While in Nairobi, Kenya on business, I visited Nairobi National Park. It was an outstanding wildlife refuge twenty miles wide by twenty five miles long containing animals of all the species of that country. Elephants, lions, tigers, giraffes, rhinos, hippopotami, and more were there to be seen. I rented a car and drove through the park, snapping pictures of most of the animals. They seemed quite tame because they received all of their food from the park personnel.

There were many winding roads throughout the park so that you could drive up close to the animals to take pictures from your car. I wanted to get a close-up of a pride of lions about thirty yards from the road. I stopped and waited a while hoping they would move closer to my car. The lions kept their distance. I decided I needed to be a little closer to the lions to get the best picture. I got out of the car and took a few steps when a big lion started running at me. I ran back, jumped into the car and moved on to another area of the park with different animals.

INDIAN PEOPLE WITH NO PLACE TO GO

The next day I had an appointment with the commercial attaché at the United States Embassy. Upon arrival, I noticed that a line stretching more than a block queued at the British Embassy next door. With our meeting concluded, I asked the attaché why so many Indian people were lined up at the British Embassy. He told me the sad story. When Britain had ruled Kenya, many educated people were brought in from India in to do the administrative work. Once Kenya gained their independence from Britain in 1963, the Kenyans started replacing the Indian administrative personnel with Kenyans who were gradually becoming educated.

The Indians, who were in Kenya on work visas, were given a deadline to leave the country. India, which had population problems, refused to allow the Indians to return. The British also refused to let the Indians immigrate to Britain. I was never able to find out what ever happened to the thousands of Indians who were caught in this immigration trap.

BOGOTA, COLOMBIA AND THE $10 ROLEX

On a visit to Bogota, Colombia, I visited a restaurant near my hotel. On my return to the hotel, I was approached by a street vendor selling watches. Most of the merchandise purveyed by these people was stolen. I made it a practice not to encourage them by buying anything. However, he showed me a Rolex watch that appeared to be in excellent condition. I told him I was not interested. As we walked along he kept lowering the price. Finally he got down to ten dollars. In order to quiet his begging I agreed to give the vendor ten dollars for the watch. It was running with the correct time and looked real. The next morning I looked at the watch and saw that it had stopped running during the night. I tried to wind it but it would not wind. I decided to keep it anyway. By the time I returned to Dallas, the numbers were falling off of the dial.

KIDNAPED IN LAGOS, NIGERIA

Nigeria was both one of the most oil rich and poverty laden nations in Africa. They had to have a good air traffic system to allow outside experts to manage their oil exploration and production. TI airport radars were a basic part of this air traffic infrastructure. I made several trips there to discuss the system performance and upgrades.

On a previous visit I'd had the pleasure of dining with Robert McNamara, who was then the president of the World Bank. We discussed potential loans that might be available to Nigeria for upgrades to their air traffic control system.

Prior to my last visit there, I asked my CIA contact to visit my office to discuss the trip. He warned me that the Nigerian government was in a state of chaos. The entire law enforcement system was so corrupt that no one was safe. I had already discussed the trip with the United States commercial attaché. He advised me to check into the Marriott Hotel and have the hotel arrange my transportation. He cautioned me against doing anything but visiting my Nigerian government contacts or the United States Embassy.

Once in the country, my visit to our embassy lasted so long that my hotel transportation had returned to the hotel without me. The embassy was only one mile from my Marriott Hotel, both being on the main Lagos Boulevard. Seeing that I was stranded, the embassy receptionist ordered a taxi to return me to the Marriott. The taxi arrived and it had a rather large rider in the front seat. The taxi smelled like alcohol. About two blocks from the Marriott, the driver turned right, getting off of the main boulevard.

I immediately said to the driver, "Turn around, this is not the way to get to the Marriott."

He replied in his very poor English, "We take shortcut."

He drove on for three blocks to a crowded red light and

cross street, continuing to ignore my instructions. Soon he had to stop, as cars were sitting on all sides of the taxi blocking us in. When he stopped, I threw a twenty dollar bill over the front seat, opened the rear door, and started running as fast as I had ever run back to the main boulevard, and back to the Marriott Hotel. I did not leave my room for the rest of the day and although I had an afternoon flight at the airport, I arrived in a Marriott limousine at nine the next morning, in order to assure that nothing would stop me from leaving Nigeria.

THE SWORDLESS BULLFIGHTERS OF PORTUGAL

On a visit to Portugal, I was looking for an agent to represent Texas Instruments. One of the prospective agents that I interviewed offered to give me a tour of Lisbon. We saw the modern bridges and statues of the proud country of Portugal. After a fine Portuguese lunch, he took me to see a bloodless bullfight.

With much fanfare, several matadors entered the arena, followed by a bull. After being taunted for ten minutes, the bull was clearly enraged. The matadors exited the arena and then about a dozen colorfully dressed young men entered. They lined up facing the bull, which responded by charging them. The young men tried to jump upon the Bull's head, between his horns. One man after another piled onto the attacking bull. The bull was throwing these young men off left and right all over the arena. Once thrown, the men would rush to get in line again. Finally the bull had so many men on his head and shoulders that he fell to the ground. At this point, the bull was completely exhausted and the young men declared victory over the bull.

Mel Barney

THE FAUX AIRPORT RADAR IN ANKARA

Most of the airports I visited in the world were equipped with Texas Instruments airport surveillance radars. If I had time, I usually checked with the local civil aviation authorities about their radar's performance. I would ask how the radar was operating and if they needed any help from Texas Instruments. I once landed in Ankara, Turkey, and as we approached I could see that the Texas Instruments radar antenna was rotating. I asked for permission to go up to the tower and talk to the air traffic controllers using the radar.

To my surprise, when I asked them how it was working, they admitted that the radar was not working and had not worked for several weeks. I asked why then was the antenna still spinning. They said they had been instructed to keep the antenna on so that it would rotate and people would think that the airport radar was working. I talked to the authorities about this problem and we arranged to have some Texas Instruments radar technicians come to Ankara and help them fix the radars.

When Texas Instruments sold airport radar to a foreign country, we trained their technicians very well. When the technicians returned to their country they had learned so much more about electronics, that they could earn a lot more money from someone else other than the government job of maintaining the airport radars. This was a problem Texas Instruments faced frequently. It was also faced by many other technology companies when they sold equipment overseas.

HONG KONG RICKSHAW

In Hong Kong, I got off of the plane and took a ferry to the city center. I then debated whether to take my usual, taxi, or to try riding in a rickshaw to my hotel. I opted for my first rickshaw ride. I hailed an operator, asking him to take me to the Marriott Hotel. As I boarded, he put my bags on a rack in the back and off we went. The hotel was only about two blocks away, so there was little time to enjoy the ride.

At the hotel, the operator unloaded my bags and said, "Twenty dolla."

I said, "You have only taken me two blocks, how could it possibly be twenty dollars?"

He replied, "Twenty dolla."

I called the hotel doorman over, hoping to get his assistance in this negotiation. He advised, "Pay him twenty dollars. If I call the police, you will lose."

I paid the twenty dolla, and learned a valuable lesson: always negotiate first.

LAWN CROQUET AND THE TAJ MAHAL IN INDIA

I learned from my CIA contact in Dallas that India was considering a completely new air traffic control system. In order to successfully compete, we needed to pick a top-notch agent to represent Texas Instruments in India. I called the United States commercial attaché in India and asked him to give me the names of several good agents who had represented American companies there. He gave me three good contacts. After looking at the background and the companies they had represented, I decided my best bet was to consider one in New Delhi. I contacted the agent and set up a visit to discuss the business with him directly.

The motivation for the agents that we hired was to win a contract and then get a percentage of the contract as their reward for assisting with the proposal and the sale of the program. At that time, it was acceptable to give the agent from five percent to ten percent of the total contract value if we won the contract.

I flew to India, and the contact met me at the airport and took me to my hotel. The next day we discussed the prospects of the new business, how much he knew about it and what his thoughts were in terms of us presenting a winning proposal. For several days, we went over the needs of the Indian government for air traffic control radars. We discussed who the key players were in the Indian government. We discussed how well he knew these particular officials. We also discussed what he knew about the upcoming contract for this equipment. He seemed to be well connected and understood the type of equipment we were trying to sell. I decided that we would hire him as an agent and would probably bid on the India contract.

He appeared to be very wealthy as he lived in a very large house in a gated community. At that time, and I suspect today, the wealthy people all lived within gated communities.

After we had finished our work and he had been selected as our agent, he decided he would do something for me to show his appreciation. On the next Sunday afternoon, he set up a party at his rural retreat home that was attended by several dignitaries, including the ambassadors from to South Korea and Taiwan.

They had set up a course to play croquet. We played croquet and I enjoyed it but didn't do very well, having never played the game before. During the afternoon, the new

Texas Instruments agent asked me if I would like to visit the Taj Mahal. I said that would be wonderful. He told me he would have his driver pick me up the next morning and drive me to Agra, where the driver would then choose a suitable guide to show me around the Taj Mahal. Right on time the next morning, his driver picked me up in a limousine. We drove from New Delhi to Agra over a two-lane highway that had very few highway signs. The highway was clogged with ox driven carts, pedestrians, and many old clunker cars. It was a wild ride with the driver dodging road obstacles on both lanes of the highway.

The Taj Mahal is a wondrous thing to behold. I can see how it came to be regarded as one of the Seven Wonders of the World. It was built more than five centuries ago. That they managed to build a temple so tall and ornate back then is amazing. Any description that I could give would certainly not be adequate to describe just how magnificent it is.

Inside is the tomb of the Emperor's wife, who he adored and who died when she was a young lady. It was said that he grieved for the rest of his life for his beautiful young wife. As the guides will tell you the Emperor had 50 concubines constantly at his disposal. I was also taken to the other side of the Ganges where the father of the Emperor had built his own temple at an earlier time.

It was interesting to note that the sides of the main Taj Mahal building are semi-precious stones all around the periphery. The stones are imbedded in white marble. The four sides have exactly the same pattern. I bought a sample of the inlaid semi-precious stones on white marble stone.

Mel Barney

A replica of a Taj Mahal wall with inlaid
semi-precious stones

PREFERENTIAL TREATMENT
IN KINSHASA, CONGO

Even Third World countries need airports to carry on what little commerce they are able to conduct. I had heard through the USAID connections that the Democratic Republic of the Congo was trying to put in a civil aviation airport radar system. I made arrangements to fly to Kinshasa,

94

where I had arranged to meet with the United States Embassy's commercial attaché. I flew in on an airplane filled with mostly Africans dressed in traditional garb. I stood out like a sore thumb in my business suit. After we had landed and pulled up to the gate, the passengers lined up in one line to go through customs and passport control. I was about fiftieth to go through this slow process.

After only a few minutes one of the locals came up and told me if I would use his taxi he would get me by this line. I said I may be arrested for doing something wrong. He showed me his badge, which read "Customs Director". I agreed to take his taxi. He grabbed me by the arm and took me up in front of the line. He asked me to show him my baggage, which I did.

He picked up the bags and signaled for me to follow him. He had an old Volkswagen. I paid him for the taxi ride, and made arrangements for him to take me to the embassy the next day. I walked out of the hotel and looked at some of the street vendor wares. There were all kinds of animal skins, tiger heads, and other objects that the poachers had taken from the jungles surrounding Kinshasa. I bought an elephant tusk with an African face carved on the front as a souvenir.

The next day the taxi driver picked me up and took me to the United States Embassy, where I met with the commercial attaché. He told me that the Democratic Republic of the Congo was going to purchase an air traffic control radar system, but he had just received some very good inputs that indicated that a French company had close ties to the head of their civil aviation organization. He suggested that the expense to Texas Instruments, of trying to bid on this particular contract was not worth the gamble to win it. I thanked the attaché, packed my bags and my souvenir tusk and headed back to Dallas.

Mel Barney

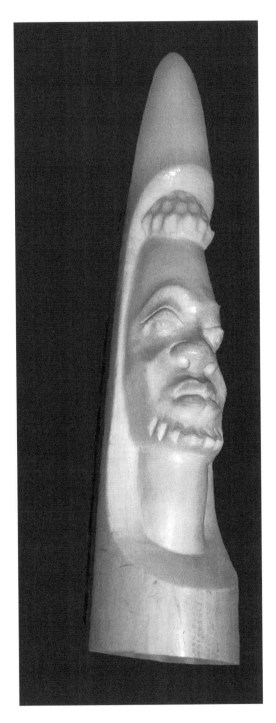

Carved elephant tusk from Kinshasa

LIQUOR AND PLAYBOY MAGAZINES IN SAUDIA ARABIA

I received word from friends in the FAA that Saudi Arabia was planning a new airport system for Mecca. Mecca is considered the holiest city in Islam, and hundreds of thousands of Muslims visit annually as a pilgrimage. I contacted my CIA friend in Dallas to advise me on this trip. He gave me many dos and don'ts about visiting Saudi Arabia. Included among his suggestions was not to take in any sexy magazines, such as Playboy, nor any type of liquor.

I flew into Jetta and was met by a prince of the royal family. There are hundreds of princes of the royal family. I was taken to the hotel, then later picked up and taken to his palace. We discussed the Mecca airport project and the timing of the program. He told me he was planning a party in my honor in his palace that evening. He said we would finish our discussions of the airport project the next day. I was taken back to my hotel for a brief respite before the festivities.

I was cordially met as I entered the party. To my surprise the entertainment for the party was American music and musicians. The liquor was flowing as many beautiful women roamed around the room flirting with all the men, including me. I can truthfully say that throughout all of my travels, I conducted myself as a faithful husband. Although this was a tempting environment, I maintained my composure. While the other men at the party drank heavily, I nursed one scotch and soda all night.

The Prince had scheduled a meeting for the next morning. I met with the potential Texas Instruments agent in his palace, and we discussed terms for an agreement in which he would represent Texas Instruments in Saudi Arabia. His terms were for 25 percent of any contract that Texas

Instruments got for the Mecca airport radar program. At Texas Instruments, the guidelines for paying agents in foreign countries stipulated that agents receive no more than ten percent of the program value.

The United States government had set up the ten percent guideline to prevent the agency from providing kickbacks to foreign governmental officials. Other countries such as Italy, Spain, and France had no such guidelines. In some cases this caused Texas Instruments and other American companies to lose big contracts in other countries.

Since we could not agree on the agent's commission rate, we ended our negotiation and I left Saudi Arabia without the prospect of winning their air traffic control radar system contract.

BRAZILIAN WORLD CUP
BEACH CELEBRATION

Roberto Frischer was the Texas Instruments agent in Brazil in 1970. Brazil had just opened their new capital in Brasilia, where an international airport was being built. Another TI engineer, Larry Reppert, and I went to Brazil and visited Roberto in Rio. Our plans were to write a proposal to Brazil for their radar for the new airport.

Roberto had visited Texas Instruments in Dallas and I had taken him out to dinner along with my wife Carolyn. He was one of the best agents we had overseas and was a personal friend. As a favor, Roberto presented me with a beautiful topaz and also a beautiful jade ring for Carolyn.

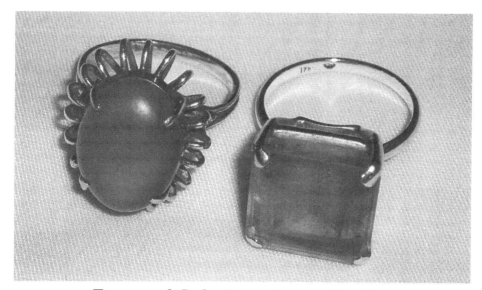

*Topaz and Jade rings given to Carolyn
from Roberto Frischer*

Roberto was a very interesting person. He had been a colonel in the Luftwaffe during World War II. He'd escaped from an Allied prison and managed to settle in Brazil. He told me that many German military people had escaped to Brazil from Allied prisons. Brazil was neutral during World War II. He had built a profitable business in Brazil by representing countries all over the world. He had a beautiful Brazilian wife.

Roberto had reserved rooms for Larry and me facing the beautiful Copacabana Beach. He took us to see some of the most outstanding sights around Rio de Janeiro including Sugarloaf Mountain, the Christ the Redeemer statue on Mount Corcovado, and Ipanema Beach, as well as several fine night clubs.

We worked for four long days on the airport proposal. During this period the World Cup soccer championship was being held in Mexico City. Brazil had their famous soccer player, Pele, and they were competing with Italy. Brazil won the match, beating Italy four to one. Roberto asked if we wanted to go down to the Copacabana beach and celebrate this victory with the Brazilians.

As it happened, at that time the Brazilians were having difficulties with the British based on problems they had on the soccer field. Roberto warned us that if anyone heard us speak, we should very promptly tell them that we are American, not British. The six hour beach celebration featured dancing, singing, music, and drinking loads of booze.

The Brazilian Air Force put on a thrilling air show doing barrel rolls and other very low flying aerobatics right atop the Brazilians celebrating on the beach. The United States Air Force would never be allowed to perform such dangerous aerobatics over such a large crowd. This was the first time that I realized that soccer (or futebol as they call it) was more of a worldwide team sport than the sports we commonly watch in the United States, like baseball, football, and basketball.

Ultimately TI won the contract and I visited Brazil several times over the next two years.

MANAUS OPERA HOUSE IN BRAZIL

On a return trip from Buenos Aires, Argentina, I stopped at Manaus, which is way up on the Amazon River in Brazil. There is an opera house in this isolated city which was built more than 100 years ago when the rubber boom brought prosperity to the area. I cannot recall the name of the opera I attended, but will never forget the ornately beautiful building.

Manaus is located along a part of the Amazon River where piranha fish are plentiful. Piranha are ugly fish was big teeth and they attack and consume other living animals, including people. I bought a stuffed piranha from a taxidermist and brought it home as a souvenir.

LAKE EYRE BELOW SEA LEVEL LAKE IN AUSTRALIA

Of all of the places I visited, Australia was the place where I felt most at home. Australians seemed to think and act more like Americans than anywhere else I visited. Texas Instruments had a plant in Adelaide that I had the opportunity to visit. One of my Australian TI friends took me on a sightseeing tour of the area. It was so interesting to see the many different animals, most of which were fairly tame. Kangaroos had no fear of people. One interesting point to me was Lake Eyre which was located about one hundred miles from the Great Australian Bight (bay). The lake is substantially below sea level and is located in an arid part of Australia. I asked my friend if they had ever considered digging a canal from the sea to the lake. He said there had been some talk, but it was a very low priority.

TYPHOON IN MANILA

In early July of 1971, I traveled to Manila to discuss TI products with the Philippine government and potential agents. I checked in with the United States embassy and talked to the commercial attaché. I then talked to people in the Philippine government. There appeared to be several TI products of potential interest to the Philippine government.

I met with several potential TI agents. One had lots of experience. We discussed potential business and what percent his fee would be for helping TI pursue these business opportunities. He appeared to be the best candidate so I selected him to represent TI. We finished our discussion and he asked me if I'd ever been to a cockfight and would I like to see one. I said no, but I would like to see one.

On the way to the cockfight he showed me the Jeep factory where they converted jeeps to small buses. When World War II ended, the U.S. government left thousands of jeeps in the Philippines. The Filipinos had taken these jeeps, altered the rear end of the Jeep, added stronger suspension springs, and put a little covered section in the back that would seat six people. As you drove around Manila, you saw hundreds of these small buses, all painted in various picturesque colors, driving the roadways filled with passengers. The way the transit system worked was that an operator would buy a jitney (small converted Jeep bus) and go find people who wanted to travel from one area to another.

At the cockfight arena we saw dozens of cocks in cages all with razor-sharp blades on one of their legs. The operator of the cockfight would place two of the armed roosters into a pen approximately 15 feet square. The roosters would start fighting the minute they were let out of their cages. They would fight for several minutes, until one of them had killed the other. It was a bloody thing to watch and I never attended another cockfight.

I finished my business on 13 July, and returned to the hotel. The hotel advised that there was a typhoon approaching Manila and would arrive early the next day. They instructed everyone to come downstairs to the lobby when the typhoon arrived. The next morning, they instructed me to come downstairs, as the typhoon was nearing. The elevators were not working, so I went down the stairwell from my eighth-story room. The lobby was full and the power went out shortly after the typhoon struck.

We were in the lobby at least 15 hours before power was restored. The typhoon had damaged the hotel significantly. The hotel had a dance floor on the top with all the band instruments including the piano. The hurricane had blown all of these instruments off of the roof of the hotel. It had also twisted the hotel so that you could see cracks as you went up the stairs to your room. The people staying in the hotel were isolated for at least 24 hours without food, communication, beds, or water. Of course my flight had been canceled, but I managed to catch a flight out of Manila two days later.

MADAGASCAR

On one of my business trips, I visited the island of Madagascar. Madagascar is a large island off of the East Coast of Africa. I was just trolling for business with no particular objective in mind. The biggest industry is tourism, and the country looks mostly like a jungle. Like the Galapagos Islands off the west coast of South America, it has many species of animals not seen anywhere else in the world. There are 75 different species of animals that are unique to this large island. One of the most plentiful was the lemur.

REYKJAVIK

On one of my trips, I flew Icelandic Airlines. On the way home I stopped at Reykjavik for a couple of days. It is a very interesting place. The volcanoes on the island provide the whole of Iceland with a continuous supply of steam. The steam is used to generate electricity, to provide a water supply, and to provide heating for the residents of this very large island. One of the big industries in Iceland is growing sheep. At that time you could get excellent prices on all types of wool clothing. I brought home sweaters for all members of the family and they lasted many years.

BANGKOK

In Bangkok, TI had an excellent agent. This agent had been a Buddhist monk. He told me all about the activities of Thailand during World War II. He said that when the Japanese came to invade, Thailand opened its borders to welcome them in. The Buddhist attitude was come on in, then once you get tired you'll go home. He told me that it was common for young Thai men to serve a few years as monks then return home to a normal lifestyle.

The Thailand Air Force was planning to update many of its aircraft and aircraft facilities. They were interested in TI's radars, missiles, and other military products. The TI agent asked me to invite high-level TI officials to visit Bangkok and discuss their needs.

I went back to Dallas and discussed the requirements of the Thailand Air Force, and I invited the three vice-presidents, including Ray McCord, Grant Dove, and one other to make the visit to Bangkok. All agreed, and we made the trip, and discussed contributions that TI might make to the Thailand Air Force upgrade program. There were many good opportunities for TI in Thailand.

Apparently the Thailand Air Force wanted to impress the TI officials. They planned a very elaborate dinner for the group. When we entered the exotic restaurant, there were about 15 beautiful young ladies lined up in the restaurant. We were told to pick a young lady to be our individual waitress for the evening. We were then led into a private room which had no chairs or tables, but large cushions everywhere. We were told the ladies would serve us whatever we chose, including massages. We were then given a menu of all finest Thai dishes. We would order, and our appointed waitress would go fill the order. We had terrific dinners and I can say that none of the TI group participated in any activity that could be considered inappropriate.

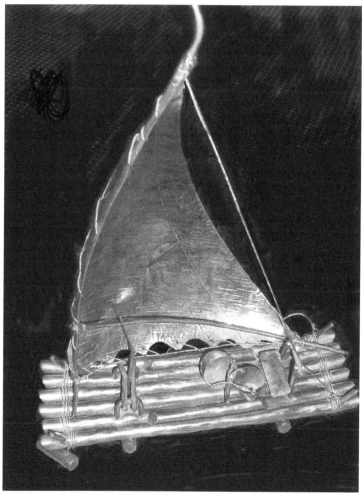

Souvenir raft from Thailand given to me
by my Buddhist friend.

As a further treat for the visiting group, we were taken on a large tourist canoe down the Chao Phraya River. Many large resort hotels are along the river. Interestingly, dozens of very young Thai swimmers followed the canoe as it toured up and down the river. This was because tourists would throw money out in the water and the swimmers would dive to get it. If they found coins, they would come up and hold the coins in the air. I was surprised by how many of the swimmers were able to find the coins.

TOKYO

TI had a marketing engineer in Tokyo who invited me to several interesting activities including a trip to the Ginza. I had been flying for about eight hours and he first took me to a Japanese massage parlor where I got a relaxing body massage. We had a late lunch and discussed TI business activities in Japan. He took me to the Ginza. The Ginza was a place where the businessman went after a busy day at the office to relax and meet women. In Tokyo, I was impressed by the short time it took to ride their high-speed rail from Narita Airport to the center of Tokyo. I bought a gold plate at Tokyo as a souvenir.

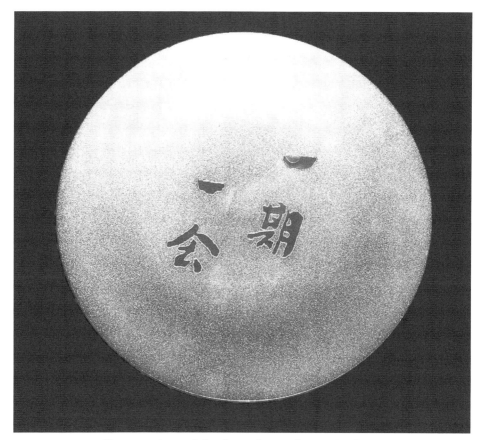

Souvenir gold plate bought in Tokyo.

SINGAPORE

I traveled through Singapore several times during my visits to Asia. I enjoyed the park in the middle of the city, where in the evening they would set up tents and serve food cooked on the spot. They would serve beef on a stick, and all types of foods including fresh vegetables and desserts. Singapore is an intriguing place. The population is about one third English, one third Malaysian, and one third Chinese. They have one of the most efficient law enforcement agencies in the world. You just do not break the law in Singapore.

Mel Barney

MUNICH

Munich was one of my favorite places to visit. We had a radar contract with a major German manufacturer when I traveled there. The most striking place I found in the city was the Deutsches Museum. It is one of the world's largest technology museums. Munich also has a rapid and efficient transportation system.

Our European marketing engineer took me to nearby Garmisch-Partenkirchen several times over the years. I greatly enjoyed visiting the scenic little town where General Eisenhower had a terrific ski resort built for the Allied Servicemen after World War II.

LONDON

I was able to take Carolyn along on many of the trips with me. Our favorite place to travel together was London with its theaters, wonderful sights, and people who spoke English. We roamed the country by rail and car from the beaches of Brighton, to Bath, to Edinburgh. Once, on a train trip from London to Edinburgh an Englishman told us the whole story of Hadrian's Wall. Hadrian's Wall was built by the Romans, and it stretches all the way across England near the Scotland border.

The first time I went to London, I got on the airplane and recognized Mr. Pat Haggerty, the president of TI, on the airplane. I had been at TI only three years then and figured he would not know me.

I approached him and said, "Mr. Haggerty, you don't know me, but…"

He interrupted, "Yes, I know you. You are Mel Barney and you're going to visit British Aircraft Corporation (BAC) to try to sell them the forward-looking radar for their SR-2 airplane. "

Mr. Haggerty was one of the finest gentlemen and presidents of a large corporation that I ever knew. My meetings went well on that trip. The TV series Dallas was very popular in England at that time and all of the BAC engineers wanted to visit Dallas, and some of them did get to visit.

My friends at the British Aircraft Corporation wanted me to get a taste of a typical old English hotel. It was a wonderful experience. The meals were served to all at the same time. Everyone sat looking at a stage featuring musical entertainment. After several days I came down with a bad cold. I could not get my room warm.

I went to the desk and asked, "Can you please turn up the heat in my room?"

The gentleman behind the desk said in a sarcastic English way, "Sir, if you will put a shilling in the meter on your heater, then you will get heat."

I finished my business and returned to Dallas.

I was asked by the Royal Air Force to visit one of their secret air force operations at an air base close to London. They wanted to exchange classified radar information. (The English did invent radar.) I got permission to exchange information with them. I traveled to their airfield close to London and we had a good exchange of secret technical information. I returned to my hotel in London.

The next morning I was preparing to return to Dallas, when I discovered that I had a British secret document in my brief case. I was almost in a state of panic because getting caught with that document would mean big trouble for me. I went to the U.S. Embassy and told the military attaché, what happened. He took the document and told me do not worry he would take care of the matter.

One of the best trips Carolyn and I had to England was

a vacation to see theater shows and to visit Scotland. At that time you could fly to London to see live theater for less than you could travel to New York to see Broadway shows. In London you could often go to a theater a few hours before the performance and buy discounted tickets. On this trip, we'd made reservations to see The Phantom of the Opera and the longest play running in London: Mousetrap. We saw several other shows as well.

After attending the shows, we caught a train for Scotland. We settled into our comfortable sleeping compartment and woke up the next day in Edinburgh, Scotland. We then enjoyed tours of the area, including a visit to Edinburgh Castle.

I have already mentioned my aversion to flying in helicopters. On the return from one trip, I had a stop in London which necessitated a transfer from Heathrow to Gatwick Airport. In order to make this change in time for my connecting flight, I had to take a helicopter. Despite the thick blanket of fog I'd noticed upon landing, I reluctantly boarded the helicopter to Gatwick. We waited after being seated, but the helicopter stayed put. Finally the captain came on the intercom and announced that the fog was too thick and we could not take off. He said we would wait to see if the fog lifted soon so we could start our flight. Finally we took off and I made my connection, but I never scheduled another commercial helicopter flight.

COLLAPSED BRIDGE IN CURACAO

Off of the coast of Venezuela lie the islands of Aruba, Bonaire, and Curacao. Their economies are primarily supported by resort hotels and gambling establishments. TI had a microchip factory in Curacao which I was invited to visit. Curacao has a beautiful bay named St. Anna Bay. The bridge over the entrance to the bay had to be long and high. The first bridge (Queen Juliana) was being built to attract tourists after World War II. According to my TI host, the cables that were supporting the suspension span on one side of the bridge became corroded from salt water. The cables broke and both ends of the bridge collapsed into the bay. The Queen Juliana was rebuilt and completed in 1974.

DO NOT DRINK AND DRIVE IN OSLO

In Oslo, I discussed the equipment TI had there and future business opportunities with our agent. He took me out to dinner. When he arrived at my hotel to pick me up I saw that he had a driver. He explained that in Norway, if you are stopped and have any smell of alcohol on your breath, you have your driver's license suspended forever. Along with dinner, we drank aquavit, a traditional flavored spirit. He told me that after the Norwegian aquavit was brewed, the bottles were placed on ships that traveled around the world. The rolling of the ships added a distinctive taste to the liqueur.

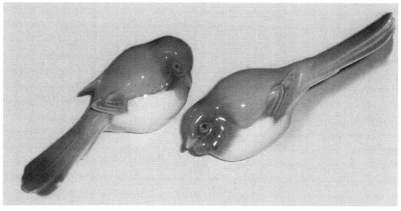

Norwegian optimist and pessimist bird figurines

He then gave me several bottles along with two other gifts. One was the Norwegian 1971 Christmas Plate and the other was a set of beautiful optimist and pessimist bird figurines.

Norwegian Christmas Plate

BE WARY OF TOUR GUIDES IN ITALY

We bought a tour package to take the family to Europe. Italy was one of the destinations. Included in the Italian tour package was a trip from Rome to Naples, Capri, and Pompeii. The tour guide had our bus group stop at so many souvenir shops that by the time we got to Pompeii it was almost dark. When we stopped at the souvenir shops the tour guide would stay behind while we got back on the bus. She was getting kickbacks from the shop owners. Finally, the driver pulled up to the gate at Pompeii, which had already been locked.

The bus driver turned up the headlights and our tour guide proudly announced, "Here is Pompeii," which was all we got to see of it.

However, on a later trip to Italy we did spend a whole day looking over the ruins of Pompeii caused by the eruption of Mount Vesuvius in 49 AD.

SHOT AT IN JAKARTA

In discussions with my friends at IBM, I learned that Indonesia was planning a new airport radar system for the Jakarta International Airport. They mentioned that they had a very good agent representing them in Jakarta. They invited me to contact him to see if he would like to represent Texas Instruments. The equipment that IBM was selling to Jakarta was not in competition with our product.

I asked my CIA friend to advise me concerning this trip to Indonesia. He did so, further discussing some things he would like for me to observe. He warned me about a terrorist group that was active throughout Indonesia, telling me not to be caught out alone.

I contacted the IBM agent in Jakarta and ask if he would be interested in being an agent for Texas Instruments. He said he certainly would be interested, and suggested that I bring my golf shoes. I agreed and we set a date for my visit. He met me at the airport and dropped me off at the Intercontinental Hotel, which was on the main boulevard in Jakarta. We met the next morning and discussed the specifics of an agent agreement between him and Texas Instruments. He provided me with specifications and other requirements of the proposal that would be submitted to the Indonesian civil and aviation officials.

With our information exchanged and business agreements made, we decided to play golf the next morning. He picked me up and took me to his country club, which had a very fine clubhouse and golf course. We played a round of golf, had a snack then drank a beer. He then took me back to the hotel.

By late afternoon, I had cleaned up and gotten dressed. As I stood in the doorway to my balcony facing the main Jakarta boulevard, I heard what sounded like a gunshot and heard a thud from inside the room. I looked up and saw a hole in the ceiling. I dropped to the floor, grabbed the phone, and called the front desk to tell them what had happened. They sent a detective up. When he saw the bullet hole in my ceiling, they moved me to a room across the hall and on a lower floor. I had dinner in my room, checked out of the hotel the next morning and flew back to Dallas. Under the circumstances we decided not to bid on the Jakarta International Airport.

BEIRUT:
"TAKE ME TO THE AIRPORT NOW"

I got a letter from a person in Beirut suggesting that there was an airport radar requirement in Lebanon. He wanted to be the TI agent. I talked to my CIA friend and asked if he knew of any airport activity in Lebanon. He said that he did not. I told him about the letter I had received and asked him what he thought I should do. This was after my Lagos kidnaping experience, so I was cautious. He suggested that the next time I was near Lebanon I should arrange to meet the letter writer in the airport.

Several weeks later I was traveling to Iran so I called the potential agent and suggested that he meet me in the Beirut airport so that we could discuss the Lebanon airport project. He spoke fairly good English and seemed intelligent. I told him that I would arrive at the Beirut airport around eight in the morning. We could talk at the airport until I caught my flight out at around six that evening. He agreed.

When I arrived he gave me a beautiful brass tea pitcher. We discussed the project over a cup of coffee and then he said the airport food was no good and we should go to a nice Lebanese restaurant nearby. I protested, telling him I did not want to leave the airport. He insisted it was only a short distance to the restaurant. He seemed like such a nice gentleman, I finally agreed to go to the restaurant. It was much further away than a few blocks. The restaurant was in a business district of Beirut. We had a good lunch and discussed all of the TI agent and radar requirements.

By one o'clock I started getting nervous and told him I wanted to return to the airport. He said we had plenty of time. He kept putting me off every time I mentioned the airport. By three o'clock I was very agitated.

I caught his eye, firmly asserting, "I want to go to the airport now."

When he stalled again, I grabbed my briefcase and suitcase and ran out of the restaurant. Fortunately there were several taxi cabs on the street. I hopped in the first one and told him to take me to the airport fast. He did rush me to the airport and I left Lebanon for the last time.

*Brass tea pitcher I received
from Lebanese potential agent in Beirut*

BIG BUSINESS WITH THE SHAH OF IRAN

I made three or four trips to Iran during the reign of the Shah in the early 1970s. TI had a lot of business with Iran including seismic, semiconductor, and military products. We had a senior marketing engineer, Richard Stripling and his wife, Betty, living in Teheran. One of the first problems Richard encountered was not receiving his mail including his paycheck. He caught up with the postman one day and asked why he had not been receiving his mail.

The postman told him, "When you start paying me in riyals each month, then you will get your mail." With no other options available, Richard bribed the postman and started getting his mail.

Richard heard that Iran was buying new airport radar for the Shiraz airport. I flew to Shiraz to discuss the airport radar requirements with the local officials. Those officials suggested that while in the area I should visit nearby Persepolis, which had been the Persian capital during the reign of Darius in 339 A. D. When Alexander the Great invaded that area he had ravaged Persepolis and burned down a part of their huge office structure. The building was reported to have had more than three thousand employees who governed the territory. Alexander the Great had torched the building in revenge for the destruction the Persians inflicted on Athens many centuries prior. Persepolis was fascinating.

On my flight back to Tehran I noticed what appeared to be ripple bombing holes going on for miles in the Iranian desert. I asked Richard about these holes and he said that there is a constant down slope of the terrain from north to south. Water was the most precious liquid in earlier times. An industrious person could dig a well and make money by selling water. Once he found water he could dig another well south of the first one, tunnel back to the first well, and extend the water producing area. Year after year additional wells were dug with tunnels back to the well to the north. These wells were called qanats. There was an old Iranian saying that there are no old qanat diggers. The reason was that by the time he had tunneled back to the up-hill water source, a young qanat digger would have gotten killed by another trying to steal his water system.

Teheran had amazing bazaars selling everything you could imagine. The bazaars, which covered several blocks, were laid out in large clusters of merchants selling mostly handmade items. The exchange rate between the riyal and the dollar was very favorable then. Things were unbelievably inexpensive for people with dollars.

Samovar purchased in Tehran

I had some experience with Westminster chime wall clocks. You could buy one in the bazaars for around twenty five dollars. These clocks were made mostly in Germany. When the Iranians got electricity they sold their wind up clocks and many of the clocks showed up in the bazaars. I bought twenty clocks and shipped them to my Dallas address. I also bought a Samovar. I was able to sell enough clocks to make the venture profitable.

KARACHI COBRA CHARMER

Karachi had TI airport radar. I visited the airport tower and everything appeared to be in order. As I returned to the hotel I saw a crowd of people in front of the hotel. I went over and saw a Pakistani wearing a turban and playing a flute. He was sitting in front of a wicker basket. As he blew the flute a cobra raised his head out of the basket and seemed to sway along with the music. The man would hold the flute in one hand and slowly rotate his other hand over the cobra's head. He had a tip basket in front of where he was sitting. Coins were tossed into the basket. The cobra never struck at the flute player. I bought the tortoise shell figurines to remember the trip.

Tortoise shell figurines from Karachi

BUDAPEST: A BEAUTIFUL OLD CITY

I went to Budapest to discuss an airport improvement program. I met with civil officials and they indicated that the TI airport radar was not the kind of equipment they were looking for. I took a couple of tours of the beautiful old city, bought a souvenir jewel box for Carolyn and proceeded to my next destination.

Jewel box from Budapest

NORTH KOREAN THREAT DETOURS FLIGHT

One of my longer trips included Bangkok, Manila, Hong Kong, Singapore, Kuala Lumpur, Singapore, Taipei, and Seoul, South Korea. On the segment from Taipei to Seoul the flight was scheduled to arrive several hours after dark. The weather was terrible and the airplane was bouncing around uncomfortably, somewhat above the one martini level.

We were about thirty minutes from landing in Seoul when the Captain came on the speaker to announce that due to the weather we would have to enter a holding pattern north of the Seoul airport. He then said that considering the bad weather and the potential of flying into a "North Korean threat zone," he'd need to divert the flight to an airport in southern Japan. He promised that the airline would take us to a hotel and provide meals before returning to the airport the next morning to continue on to Seoul.

Before leaving Dallas, I had a long session about the trip with my CIA contact. He gave me some guidance about business activities in these countries, some things I should be aware of from a safety stand point, and some of the things he would like to know about general activities. In South Korea, he was interested in how the people that I dealt with felt toward the United States.

In Seoul I talked to a potential TI agent, the United States commercial and military attachés, and the Civil Aviation Agency personnel about updates on their plans for their airport in Seoul. It turned out to be a good trip because we sold the new radar for their airport.

TWO MISERABLE TRIPS
ARRIVED LATE, NO HOTEL

I had one of the best secretaries in all of TI named Pat Locurcio. She took care of my complicated airline and hotel reservations, meeting schedules, and other details for the long trips I was taking. On trips to Santo Domingo and Caracas other people's mistakes caused me to spend a miserable night in each of these cities. I always had hotel reservation confirmations or someone I knew to pick me up and take me to my hotel.

I had a written hotel confirmation number for a visit to Santo Domingo, Dominican Republic. I was to meet with the United States commercial attaché. When I arrived in the late afternoon, the hotel manager said that even though I had a valid confirmation number, the hotel was full so I could not get a room. He suggested that I spend the night in the gambling casino that was part of the hotel. After arguing with the manager, I realized that I would not win. I had traveled enough to know that you do not want to get arrested in a foreign country, so I decided to live with the situation. I got permission to sleep out in one of the cabanas next to the swimming pool. It was hot and uncomfortable. There was continuous noise from people making love. The next morning I caught a taxi to the airport and returned to Dallas.

We had an airport radar in Caracas, Venezuela. We also had an agent. The Venezuela government was planning to replace the older TI radar with a new one. I had talked to the agent and he offered to pick me up at the airport at a specific time and date. He said he would make hotel reservations for me. I arrived at the airport in the late afternoon. The agent was not there to meet me. I tried calling him but got no answer. I took a taxi for the long ride from the airport to the city center. Every first class hotel we went to was full.

Finally, the taxi driver said, "I know of a cheap hotel that will have a place for you to sleep." Having no other choice I told him to take me there.

They gave me a small room with no bath or air conditioning. I paid the taxi driver and gave him a big tip. I asked him to pick me up early the next morning to take me to the airport. After I returned to Dallas, I called the agent to see what had happened. He claimed that he had me arriving a day later than the date we had talked about. In any event, I assigned someone else to make the next trip to Caracas.

OTHER INTERESTING OBSERVATIONS FROM MY TRAVELS

In the Copenhagen airport they had a clever way to get passengers from gate to gate. They had large tricycles with baggage holders sitting at each gate. You got off of your flight, loaded your luggage on the tricycle and pedaled to the next gate.

The Honduran city of Tegucigalpa is located in a mountainous area. In order to build a runway they were forced to have a large mountain at one end. The terrain for the runway slopes down toward the mountain. Regardless of the wind the airplanes are forced to land toward the mountain and take off in the opposite direction from the mountain.

One of the surprising things about all of my travels was that I had to hire an interpreter in only one country. That was in Sri Lanka.

MOVE TO WASHINGTON, D. C.

In 1974, TI asked me to manage the Washington D. C. Office. The assignment included overseeing the 14 marketing engineers from all areas of TI, coordinating all local activities with TI managers at other locations, making and maintaining contact with key officials who might need assistance on projects of interest to TI, entertaining guests, and overseeing the TI image in the Washington, D.C., area.

PROSPECT HOUSE

Carolyn and I found a perfect apartment on the eleventh floor of the Prospect House. This was directly in line and facing the Iwo Jima Monument, the Lincoln Memorial, the Washington Monument, and the U.S. Capitol. We had a large balcony facing these famous attractions. The building was also home to many congressmen and other officials. We had many parties there and invited friends to watch the Marines who marched around the Iwo Jima Monument every Friday evening as well as the fireworks on the Fourth of July. We could walk two blocks to attend the memorial at the Tomb of the Unknown Soldier in Arlington National Cemetery on Memorial Day.

Carolyn made friends of many neighbors, including congressmen's wives, who took her to places like the congressional building, where she dined and shopped in the Capitol Store, and the White House. She thoroughly enjoyed our years in Washington. We also attended many social events including the inauguration dances for President Jimmy Carter, and the monthly breakfasts of the Texas Congressional Delegation.

PENTAGON AND CONGRESS

My Pentagon Pass and parking sticker allowed me to visit the Pentagon any time. I recall many meetings in the Pentagon concerning existing and prospective programs of interest to TI. It was there that I got acquainted with Dr. William Perry, the secretary of defense under President Carter. Later on after I had left TI and co-founded Merit Technology Incorporated, I asked Dr. Perry to be on our board of directors.

In some cases we assisted governmental staffers with their requirements to write specifications for new programs. We would get appropriate support from Dallas and write the specifications so that they favored TI equipment.

We constantly reviewed the Commerce Business Daily and the current U.S. budget details to search for government programs that might be of interest to TI.

AMERICAN ENTERPRISE INSTITUTE

I was encouraged to meet with several lobbying organizations such as the American Enterprise Institute. Carolyn attended some of these meetings with me. Frankly, I did not enjoy this part of my work. Many of the issues discussed were not in agreement with my political philosophy. Being a staunch believer in not being tied to either the conservative or liberal parties, I found that the general philosophy of these organizations was usually too far right or left to suit me. I attended these meetings but seldom made any comments.

ENTERTAINMENT

A substantial part of my work was to entertain customers and potential customers. This included taking them on ski trips, golf tournaments, and the like. A favorite activity was to take these guests to see Mark Russell, the political satirist at the Shoreham Hotel.

Carolyn had made friends with many people in the Prospect House, in particular Mrs. Poage, who was the wife of U. S. Representative Bob Poage, from the Waco area. We had frequent weekend activities, including one trip during which the Poages took us to Gettysburg. Congressman Poage was a history enthusiast and he told us all about the battle of Gettysburg. However, between finding new business for TI, escorting company executives around Washington, managing the office with 14 marketing engineers, attending many functions which often did not interest me, and being far away from our children, I decided, with Carolyn's consent, to move back to Dallas. My basic interest was in creating, building, and selling new products.

TI'S NEW IDEA DEPARTMENT

TI had a department that concentrated on developing new products. The head of the department was Gene Helms. At that time I had an interest in physical fitness and running. I suggested to Gene that we develop an instrument, worn like a wristwatch that would provide the runner's pulse rate, time, footfall rate, and blood pressure. Gene liked the idea and provided the resources to develop the instrument.

ATHLETE'S COMPUTER

We set up a treadmill and instrumentation to test runners on it. Using volunteers we began testing devices that would measure the pulse rate, time, steps per minute, and blood pressure. We immediately ran into a problem because we found that every time the foot hit the ground, it would send as many as five G's through the body. It was impossible to distinguish between a footfall and heartbeat signals. We solved this problem by putting an accelerometer on the belt, which measured only the footfall rate. Using an autocorrelation mathematical function, we were then able to then arrive at the heart rate.

The instrument was developed and patent number 4,312,358 was awarded to me for this invention. We had four different focus groups critique the usefulness of this product. They were all positive and we started planning production of the Athlete's Computer. We had cleared all obstacles to start production except the legal department. The TI legal department killed the program because they reasoned that at least a few people would die while running and using this computer. They might sue TI for millions of dollars.

LORAN C

The TI president and several of the top vice presidents were avid sailors. The Navy had set up a program for sailors to navigate using their new LORAN C System. The TI managers wanted TI to build a LORAN C System with the latest integrated circuit technology. I was asked to set up a marketing organization to sell the new product.

Doss Dunlop was a good TI friend of mine. He, along with two others owned a 38 foot sloop. I asked Doss if he would like to take his sloop named Delilah on a cruise to test the TI 9000 LORAN C System. He said that he and another owner of the Delilah, Bill Gott and his wife Glenda were planning to sail to Clearwater, Florida. He invited me to test the TI 9000 on their return trip to Galveston. At the appointed time I flew down to meet Doss, Bill and Glenda at Key Island in the Clearwater area.

They prepared the Delilah for the trip and we headed for the harbor entrance. There was a drawbridge there for when a tall ship was entering or exiting the harbor. We set sail and Bill, who was at the helm, blew the horn. This was the normal signal for the operator to raise the drawbridge. We sailed toward the drawbridge and nothing happened. At the last minute, Bill did a 180 turn and blew the horn again several times. Finally, the drawbridge went up and we sailed out into the open Gulf of Mexico. We were on our way.

The Coast Guard had lighted buoys at specific latitudes and longitudes all over the Gulf of Mexico. We had been out of the harbor only two or three hours when I made my first test of the TI 9000. We had located a known buoy and the TI 9000 guided us correctly to it. All the way across the Gulf of Mexico the TI 9000 worked well and was simple to operate. Doss, Bill and Glenda all operated it from time to time.

Mel operating the TI9000 aboard the Delilah

On the second morning out the jib halyard came loose and got stuck on the top of the mast. Doss climbed up and freed the halyard. We were buffeted by winds of up to 40 knots for about three hours. Even Doss got seasick, but, seasoned sailor that he was, recovered rapidly. It was fortunate that Doss had been able to fix the halyard, or we could have gotten into trouble with the high winds.

All through the trip, Bill trailed a fishing line behind us. The first of the many fish he caught was a ten pound bonito. Glenda was an excellent cook and served up the bonito for dinner. At one point, Bill caught a 36 inch barracuda. Glenda served it in cheese and butter sauce, which was delicious. By the fifth day we were in line with the Mississippi. We started seeing very large oil rigs everywhere. This was a comforting sight to me.

Barracuda caught by Bill Gott

On the sixth day, we began to smell gasoline. Bill examined the engine and found gas gushing from the carburetor. We managed to clean out the bilge and fix the carburetor and we were on our way again.

They had planned to drop Glenda off at Venice, Louisiana. One can enter the Mississippi River either by the east channel, the south channel, or the west channel. Although it was not recommended by the Coast Guard, we chose to take a shortcut through the east channel. We got several miles up the channel before landing on a sandbar. We tried everything we could think of to extricate the boat, but nothing worked. Finally Bill said we would need to keg off. This involved someone getting in a dinghy, taking the anchor out to a deeper spot in the channel, dropping the anchor, and returning to the boat. At this point we would use a ratchet to pull the boat toward the anchor.

I volunteered to drop the anchor. I got into the dingy, put the anchor in my lap, and paddled out about 40 feet where we thought the water would be deeper. When I threw the anchor overboard, the anchor line caught on my life preserver and if I hadn't been very quick to lie flat in the dingy, the anchor would've pulled me down with it to the bottom of the channel. Bill and Doss carefully pulled the dinghy with me clinging to the bottom while the anchor hung over the side, back to the Delilah. We opened the fifth of scotch, and by the time we had finished it, apparently, the tide had come in and the Delilah was floating free. We backed out of the east channel, then sailed up the south channel to Venice, Louisiana where we dropped Glenda off and got supplies.

We exited the south channel and headed west. As we headed out, we saw oil rigs everywhere and finally, High Island in the distance. We knew that we were close to our destination. We were happy to be back in Texas.

Unfortunately, before we could start production on the TI 9000 another company had come up with a marine navigation system that depended on the global positioning system (GPS). Our product would not be able to compete with this new type of system in either performance or cost so the TI 9000 program was scrapped.

TOPICAL MAP PROGRAM FOR WRIGHT PATTERSON AIR FORCE BASE

The TI marketing engineer in Dayton, Ohio advised that the Air Force laboratory was interested in talking to TI and other vendors about providing a system that would receive GPS information and convert it into readable maps suitable for use in their aircraft. I knew many of the engineers in the laboratory at Dayton so TI asked me to take over the pursuit of this opportunity. TI managed to win the contract and was working on the program when its funding was cut by the Air Force.

NOT A SMART THING TO DO

I often went home to have lunch with Carolyn. One day on my way back to work, I pulled into a gas station to fill up. As I started pulling out of the parking lot, I heard a commotion and saw two ladies who had just exited the Kroger Store screaming as a man ran off with their purses. I drove toward the man and followed him down a residential street.

He ran between two houses and I got out of my car and chased him screaming, "Stop thief! Stop thief!"

It just so happened that six telephone linemen were

working between the houses where he fled. They knocked him down and held a large pipe over his head. The lineman holding the pipe, handed it to me saying, "He's yours now."

The culprit was lying on his stomach, hands and feet out-stretched. I warned him, "If you move one muscle I will drive this pipe through your head."

Fortunately, the Richardson Police had already been called and soon arrived. In about a week, I received a certificate of appreciation from the Richardson Police Department.

Crime fighter Mel's official certificate of appreciation

THE FOUNDING OF MERIT

I had some highly classified ideas that I wanted to pursue, and although TI is a wonderful company which had been good to me, I decided to try to start up a new company to develop my ideas. I retired from TI and was given a lavish retirement party.

I had conceived some specific ideas about covert penetration of enemy territory. This work required the highest level of military security. A friend and former TI coworker called Sam Smith was working for Sevin Rosen, a well-known venture capital company in Dallas. I went to Sam and we talked about my idea. Most of the work on my proposed highly classified program would be with the National Security Agency (NSA). I made a presentation of the idea to L. J. Sevin, Jon Bayless, and Berry Cash at Sevin Rosen. They liked my idea and put up one million dollars in seed money to get us started. We then took the program to Palo Alto, California and received another ten million dollars for Merit Technology Incorporated's operations.

I had nine good friends at TI who were highly educated electrical engineers that I had worked with on various programs. Over a period of nine months, I hired all of them to come to work at Merit. I'd had contact with Dr. Bill Perry, secretary of defense under President Carter, when I had been assigned to the TI Washington D. C. Office. I asked Dr. Perry to serve on our Merit Board of Directors and he accepted.

All of the engineers now at Merit had experience working at the highest levels of military security. We built a secure laboratory vault that was shielded on all sides with copper plating in order to prevent any of our classified work from being detected outside of the laboratory. With the help of Dr. Perry, I was able to visit the National Security Agency (NSA) and to secure several contracts with the agency. Once Merit performed well on these contracts, we were directed to other governmental agencies and companies with programs requiring the high level of expertise that we could offer.

When bidding on jobs, we were able to present proposals with very impressive resumes. At Merit our goal was to combine the latest technology (like the Global Position

System), computer developments, military aircraft capabilities, and information on enemy territory into a system to reduce the workloads of pilots flying into hostile territory. We planned to greatly reduce the stress of military pilots on these dangerous missions.

By 1989, I had worked continuously on high stress programs for 37 years. At age sixty one, I agreed with Carolyn that I was ready to retire. I had founded a successful company and felt that I had satisfactorily contributed my abilities and expertise to the companies that had employed me. Carolyn and I wanted to travel, enjoy our new home and spend time with our grandchildren.

At my retirement party I was presented with a plaque which reads: To Mel Barney, Founder-Merit Technology Incorporated, in Recognition of Major Contributions in the Conception, Establishment and Growth of Merit from 1984 - 1989 Board of Directors: Berry Cash, Jon Bayless, William Perry, Sam Smith

Mel Barney

PART IV

WORLD ECONOMIC WAR
(1991-2011)

RETIREMENT FUN TIME

When I retired in 1989, I planned to enjoy my family and do some things that I had not had time to do while working full-time. In this part of the book I briefly cover my retirement fun period. I then address the most serious part of the book which points out what I think is wrong with the country and what we need to do to fix it. I include many references to the previous three war periods that I have personally experienced. We won the three wars I discussed earlier, but I am afraid we may lose the world economic war we are presently fighting.

Mel Barney

DREAM HOUSE

Carolyn and I built our dream house in 1988, and I looked forward to working on it more in my retirement. My daughter, Barbara, who has a master's degree in interior design and I planned the house. I was the contractor though we hired a housing contractor to advise us and to recommend subcontractors. We picked a lot with a fantastic backyard bordering a creek and a lake. Our grandchildren are able to catch bass out of the creek. The house has many unusual features.

In 1959, Brookhaven Country Club opened in Farmers Branch, Texas. They offered lifetime memberships with no monthly dues for $1,000. I liked to play golf and they had many family activities. They had three golf courses, four swimming pools, a gym, and six tennis courts. We joined Brookhaven with a lifetime membership. The lot we bought is only three blocks away from the country club.

Tests on the lot before we started building showed that there was an underground spring about 12 feet under the lot. To ensure stability, I had 46 eighteen foot deep concrete support columns with five foot flared bottoms poured to support a post tension stressed contract slab foundation. That was in 1988 and there are no cracks anywhere in the house after 23 years.

We have two separate areas in the house and separate systems to heat and cool each area. When we have company we use both systems, otherwise we use only the system that we need in our everyday living area.

We built an upstairs dormitory primarily for the grand children. It is a room 20 feet by 30 feet with a bathroom. It has TV and many games that they can enjoy. I developed a bad knee and could not climb stairs, so we put in an elevator.

View of the beautiful backyard, creek, and lake

OTHER RETIREMENT PURSUITS

In 1990, eight friends and I formed a golf group. We played a scramble on the fourth Thursday at various golf clubs in the area. By now, our group has grown to more than 45 members who play a four man scramble on the fourth Thursday every month. In 1993 Ed Fischer, Jim Holcomb and I formed a group of these golfers to have a three day golf outing including our wives at various cities within 250 miles of Dallas. The outing is always scheduled for the Wednesday after Labor Day. We usually have about 35 couples attend these outings.

In 1990 along with Ed Fischer, and Bob Quigley, I formed a two table party bridge group for the first and second Thursday of each month. Later on we formed a similar group including some of my old TI buddies for the fourth Thursday of each month. In 1991 we formed a third Thursday poker group that included 14 players from those playing in the bridge groups.

I learned to make movies on the computer and decided to compile all of the old eight mm films that I had made and that other family members had made onto one hour long family movie. I used music recordings that I had made for Sing Along With Mel as the background music. The movie disc is programmed so that you can see the video of just one of the families or all of the families. I gave copies to each family member.

Barney family movie

On my 70th birthday, Carolyn bought me an electronic keyboard. I took lessons and learned a few songs. I began volunteering to play at senior homes in the area. I kept learning more songs. Before long I was getting calls from other senior homes offering me fifty dollars to play for their residents. I learned to play more than 70 of the old favorite songs. I made several CD's of all of the songs I had learned, and a booklet entitled Sing Along With Mel which included the words of the songs I played. I was averaging two gigs a week for about four years. I had a knee that had severely damaged cartilage which made it difficult to carry the keyboard, amplifier, and other equipment into the senior homes. I quit performing because of the bad knee. I really missed playing the keyboard so I started playing again last year.

Mel's music CD

Mel Barney

SING ALONG WITH MEL - SONGBOOK $4

BOOK "SING ALONG WITH MEL" TODAY
5-26-03

Sing Along With Mel songbook

Of all of the songs I played and sang the favorite was "Amazing Grace." Audiences never got tired of hearing about the song's author, John Newton. He had been a sea captain on a slave ship bring Africans to the new world. On his last trip he ran into a terrible storm. He thought he was going to lose his ship. He went below and prayed that if the Lord would spare his ship, he would be a servant of the Lord for the rest of his life. His ship survived the storm, and John Newton became a preacher and poet. He wrote the words to "Amazing Grace" and it was later put to music. The melody was an old American melody.

My knee problem was also interfering with my golfing so I invented, developed, and patented the LEGASSIST ™, United States Patent # 6,024,713. The device was connected to the heel of the shoe and the thigh. When the knee was bent the connecting members were shorter than when the knee was straight. When the knee was straight the connecting members were longer than the normal distance from the thigh to the heel of the shoe, thus carrying the body weight directly from the thigh to the heel of the shoe. It worked very well and I used it until I had my knee replaced in 2009.

When I played golf at Brookhaven after a big rain we found hundreds of golf balls. I built a golf ball tester to test all of these "water balls." It worked well. Brookhaven bought one and I sold several others.

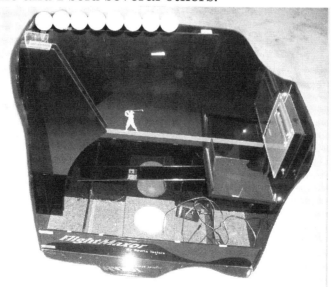

Golf ball tester

Carolyn and I are fortunate to have two children and five grandchildren. We are very proud of all of them. Barbara, our daughter, is a Dallas real estate agent who was a key contributor to the acquisition of the property for the George Bush Library. Natalie, her daughter, is a school technology facilitator. Natalie's husband Chris Hubert is a technology quality control specialist. Mike, our son, is the Technical Services Coordinator for Texas Department of Public Safety. Mike is married to Kathy Weller. Their daughter Elizabeth is married to Mark Macaluso. Both are working on PHD Programs at Texas A&M. Their oldest son Michael is married to Meghan, an attorney, and is a bond broker in Houston. Their son Daniel is a junior in computer Science at the University of Arizona. Their youngest son Tyler is a sophomore in computer engineering at LSU.

I have been heavily influenced by school teachers. Besides Miss Greer (6th grade) and my freshman high school civics teacher, my mother, wife, daughter, and granddaughter are all school teachers.

CLASS WARFARE

Since I retired I have been writing letters to the editor of the Dallas Morning News. I have had eleven published in the last three years. These letters are based on my thoughts and the philosophies I have developed through my observations and experiences all over the world, as well as my concerns about the direction our nation is headed. The middle class seem to be carrying the economic load while the poor fight our wars and the wealthy run our politics. Our big problem areas are class warfare, infrastructure, military industrial complex, and the global transition that is underway.

By the end of 1999 I realized that the country that I grew up in and prospered in was not performing in a manner that I thought would provide my children and grandchildren the opportunities that I had experienced as one of the members of what Tom Brokaw dubbed the "Greatest Generation."

All of the good momentum that made America a super power for 45 years has now been spent. We are on the verge of losing the foundation on which this country was built: the concept of shared sacrifice. If the public does not demand that the government do what is good for the citizenry, we risk the destruction of the greatest nation the world has ever known.

As a practicing engineer for 39 years, my thought process usually focuses on efficiency. The optimal system is one that rewards each component in proportion to its contribution to the entire system's operational efficiency. Generally, the most efficient system will enjoy the greatest prosperity. This applies to competing countries. One example is the winning of the cold war by the United States. We won this war because we had the best technology base.

There were two years that changed the direction of the United States in terms of its power in the world economic community. One was 1942 when the country united behind winning World War II and ending the Great Depression. Governmental actions taken that year, such as raising taxes to pay for the war and rationing food and other commodities vaulted the nation into superpower status. The key to this wonderful transition was the shared sacrifice that the government forced upon all citizens.

The other pivotal year was 1984 when the country accepted the political philosophy espoused by President Reagan's "Get the government out of my business" approach to policy. Taxes were cut along with governmental spending while the deregulation of several industries began. In my opinion, these tax breaks gradually wore down the competitive strength of the country. These changes in political direction are illustrated by the chart shown in the first part of the book.

SPEAKING UP IN PRINT

In March of 2009, The Dallas Morning News ran an article arguing that greed was the engine that drives the world's economy. Without question it is. However, greed pushes the economic engine to an intolerable speed if not governed. Americans who are able to succeed and accumulate great wealth owe it to the nation to return a commensurate portion of the wealth they have accumulated.

It seems to me that the best method of doing this is to have a graduated income tax. However, problems with this system can arise if unscrupulous people are permitted to game the system to avoid paying their fair share. This can be done by influencing congress to pass laws favoring the wealthy, investing profits overseas for tax avoidance, and hiring attorneys to gain advantage by exploiting loop holes in the income tax system. Our income tax system is good but it needs to be improved by eliminating the loop holes and simplifying the system.

Churn is the American way. Companies are born, rise, fall and die. Others come along to replace them. The country's remarkable capacity for innovation, for re-invention, is tied to its acceptance of failure. Or always has been. Without failure, the culture of risk fades. Without risk, creativity withers. If you try to save the losers, you sabotage the system.

If America loses sight of these truths, it will cease to

be itself. I do not have the financial ability or the political might to directly alter policy, but what I can do is to tell my story and to write letters to the editor. I have expressed my opinions in a number of letters which have appeared in the Dallas Morning News. These letters with the dates they were printed are shown below:

March 11, 2008:

We need interstate rail

I am a retired engineer who has investments that increase in value with the price of oil. As a patriotic U. S. citizen, it is amazing to me that the only real solution to the energy shortage is never mentioned. It is to implement an Interstate Rail System, much like President Eisenhower's Interstate Highway System. With our oil reserves, solar energy and wind turbine developments, we can be energy independent and clean.

George Melvin Barney, Farmers Branch

February 2, 2009

Gas tax could take a hike

Our relative efficiency as a nation is greatly encumbered by our low tax on gasoline.

Other developed nations have substantially higher gasoline taxes. A higher gasoline tax would raise revenue for rail and highway development and maintenance, reduce dependence on foreign oil, raise the incentives for more efficient means of transportation, and increase incentives to develop alternate energy sources.

George Melvin Barney, Farmers Branch

February 20, 2009

Trains timely in Texas

Wouldn't it be great if we could board a high-speed train in Dallas and relax for a few hours before arriving in Houston, Austin or San Antonio? Just think of the fuel savings, the increased safety, and the lack of hassle. Our representatives are deliberating this issue now. Call your representative now to help make this come true.

George Melvin Barney, Farmers Branch

March 8, 2009

Another vote for train tunnel

Re: "Dig DART tunnel under LBJ", by Joe Huber, Wednesday Letters.

This solution to the LBJ Freeway traffic problem would do more to reduce traffic congestion on LBJ than the "buggy Whip" idea of another toll road.

George Melvin Barney, Farmers Branch

March 11, 2009

All aboard for the green route

Re, "Easy riders – Kick back and chat as the Texas Eagle rolls toward San Antonio," Sunday Travel

This article will do more to improve the Dallas-Fort Worth and Texas traffic congestion, pollution, and economic problems than most of the initiatives sponsored by our political leaders.

It highlights how existing railway facilities are actually competitive in many ways with other transportation options.

George Melvin Barney, Farmers Branch

April 5, 2009

Make Medicare mandatory

Re "Some health care realism, – If we are going to have a debate, let's get our facts straight. Says David Gratzer" and "Here are five keys in getting comprehensive health care reform this year, says Ruth Markus" Monday's Viewpoints.

Neither Marcus nor Gratzer mentioned the real problem with our health care system. The real problem is that the health care insurance companies take a far greater amount of money out of the system than the value they contribute to the system.

The solution is to make Medicare mandatory for everyone who makes more than some amount, perhaps $25,000 per year. Those with less income would be covered automatically.

I believe doctors, hospitals, and citizens would all fare better under this type of system.

George Melvin Barney, Farmers Branch

DMN - March 20, 2011

Scott Burns' solutions

As a student of world economics for 60 years who has done business in more than 50 countries , I believe our country is on the brink of an Egyptian type of revolt, or a "storming of the Bastille" crisis. Scott Burns discusses the drastic actions we need to take to change our government to one that supports the needs of all of our citizens.

Each of us can support these changes by voting for candidates who are not presently incumbents and have the best interests of all of the country at heart.

George Melvin Barney, Farmers Branch

DMN - May 18, 2011

Keep LBJ all-American

Re: "No turning back – Motorists begin 5-year sacrifice until double-deck LBJ emerges" Tuesday news story.

I hear the drone of LBJ Freeway 24/7. I try to avoid LBJ at all times. I took a hammer to my toll tag, for not implementing a modern mass transit system for a dynamic economic center like north Texas.

But I resent most the fact that the LBJ fiasco will be built by a Spanish company.

George Melvin Barney, Farmers Branch

DMN - June 19, 2011

I liked Ron Paul's answers

All of the Republican debaters (6-17-11) on CNN blew smoke, equivocated, filibustered, and avoided direct answers – except one. Ron Paul was direct and brief. His most important answer was about reigning in U. S. overseas activities.

He said we could eliminate most of our national debt if we cut unnecessary bases, soldiers, troops in un-winnable wars and most other overseas operations.

George Melvin Barney, Farmers Branch

DMN - July 19, 2011

An opportunity to protest

The article on NTTA'S inability to collect toll money offers the public a way to beat the corrupt politicians. If everyone refuses to pay tolls, we will have no more toll roads.

George Melvin Barney, Farmers Branch

DMN - September 4, 2011

Economy tilts to rich

Re: "The great speed-up - The dirty secret of the jobless recovery is that while workers do more with less, corporate profits are soaring, say Monika Bauerlein and Clara Jeffery," last Sunday Points, "What a surprise – opinions run strong on tax increase," by Steve Blow, last Sunday Metro column, and "Good works, huge pay – 100 at area not-for-profits earned half a million or more, review shows," last Sunday Business.

As one who remembers the Great Depression vividly, I urge everyone to read these three pieces in last Sunday's Dallas Morning News. The U.S. economic table is getting more and more tilted in favor of the rich ruling class. The middle class and poor in our country are economically suppressed.

Please note that under Republican President Dwight Eisenhower, the highest income tax bracket was 91 percent for the highest income group. Anyone who makes less than $250,000 per year and votes for any incumbent is shooting himself in the foot.

George Melvin Barney, Farmers Branch

SOLUTIONS TO U. S. GLOBAL ECONOMIC CRISIS

The founding fathers defined the goals for the nation in the Preamble to the U. S. Constitution:

"To form a more perfect Union, establish Justice, insure domestic Tranquility, provide for the common defence, promote the general Welfare, and secure the Blessings of Liberty to ourselves and our Posterity."

The basic idea was to reward the people for their contribution to the country based upon the value of their contributions to the welfare of the nation. In return, the country would provide citizens with the protection and resources needed to fully apply their energy and intelligence and to continually improve the well being of the 'whole' country as well as the future. The intent was to create a nation where citizens were rewarded for their hard work and intelligence. They set up three interdependent branches of government to assure that a fair and representative government would also have checks and balances—that each branch would compromise and cooperate with the other for the greater good.

Our Constitution authorizes the regulation of commerce with foreign countries and between states so that the young nation might become a global competitor. It also specifically mandates the promotion of science and the arts by protecting the rights of authors and inventors, while limiting the appropriation of funds for military actions to no more than two years.

In order to accomplish the national objectives, the system has been continually refined. The franchise was extended first to former slaves, then to women. An income tax system was established to build infrastructure, fight wars, protect the citizens from those who would break the law, and perform other initiatives that were best handled on a national level.

From 1945 until the mid 1980s the U. S. was the world's undisputed and greatest military and economic superpower. The presidents from Roosevelt through Nixon along with a 'functional congress' were responsible for this enviable achievement. The decline that started in the mid 1980s from this enviable position is described in the next few paragraphs.

A chart which shows the maximum tax rate paid by the

wealthiest U. S. citizens from 1932 until 2009 is shown on the first pages of this book. Unlike sales taxes, per capita assessments and other type of revenue-generating systems, the philosophy of the income tax is to balance the tax burden so that those who can afford to pay more do and those who are subsisting on a limited income will pay less. You will note that from 1932 until 1981, the rate varied between 70% to 92% on the income of the very wealthiest Americans. Additional laws and regulations allowed them to reduce their taxes by reinvesting profits in U. S. industries. During this period the investment in U. S. infrastructure (railroads, highways, power grids, education, etc.) averaged above 6 percent of the U. S. Gross National Product (GNP). The Federal and state governments invested in many of these projects, but private companies and citizens also invested in capital expansion and industrial upgrades in order to reduce their taxable income and consequent tax liability. This investment in infrastructure is illustrated on the cover of this book. Investment in infrastructure and the tools of production almost always repay the initial investment many times over.

You will also note that between 1981 and 2009 the maximum tax rate for the wealthiest U. S. citizens varied between 28% and 35%. The investment in infrastructure starting in the mid 1980s also gradually decreased from about 5% to less than 1% today. Every American knows the deterioration of our infrastructure is mirrored in the continual degradation of our industrial base as corporations hoard their capital instead of reinvesting in equipment or the development of new products.

After the U. S. won the cold war, other nations started investing in their infrastructure, including affordable education for their citizens, while we invested in military power. The annual cost to the U. S. economy to fight unnecessary wars and keep large amounts of military equipment and personnel all over the world defeats the ability of the U. S. to compete economically with rising economic powers in Europe, South America and Asia. These countries, their industries, their entrepreneurs and their citizens now reap the benefits of high-speed rail, wide-spread and affordable alternative energy, and a highly-skilled workforce. They are developing the products of the future—products that improve the standard of living of their citizens.

President Eisenhower warned the U. S. of the 'Military Industrial Complex.' We have forgotten this warning. My whole career was devoted to building weapons of war. My role in Washington, D. C., included influencing congressional and military personnel to buy my company's equipment. I experienced how the system worked. Our political system has become so corrupted that the citizens must act to reform it.

Congress passed a law after Roosevelt was elected president for his fourth term. It limited the president to two terms. Congress should have passed a law at the same time that would have limited how many terms representatives and senators could serve. Our present congress has a shameful approval rating of 8%. The whole country knows that almost all congresspersons are more interested in enacting laws that favor their supporters and campaign donors, often at the expense of the nation and their constituents. Whether you are a Democrat or Republican, it is most likely that your congress person does not have YOUR best interest as his number one priority.

To end the Washington, D. C., corruption the U. S. citizens must:

- Stop voting for incumbents;
- Consider voting for independent candidates;
- Vote in every election for the most qualified candi-

date (who is not an incumbent);
- Continue to support term limits;
- Support nationally-financed campaigns;
- Require TV networks to provide free time for candidate debates;
- Make it a felony for any individual, company or
- interest group to donate more than $10 to a politician; and
- Limit political campaigns to 3 months.

As I stated earlier in this book, I am part of Tom Brokaw's Greatest Generation. I believe I am also part of the 'Luckiest Generation.' We experienced some bad times in our youth, but as time went on our opportunities grew and our generation enjoyed the best of times—better than any other generation in the history of mankind. I can only hope and pray that you will read this book and heed my warnings. Your government should be working toward U. S. infrastructure, not military domination.

Mel Barney

APPENDIX

INVICTUS

William Ernest Henley

Out of the night that covers me,
Black as the pit from pole to pole,
I thank whatever gods may be
For my unconquerable soul.

In the fell clutch of circumstance
I have not winced nor cried aloud.
Under the bludgeonings of chance
My head is bloody, but unbowed.

Beyond this place of wrath and tears
Looms but the horror of the shade,
And yet the menace of the years
Finds, and shall find me, unafraid.

It matters not how strait the gate,
How charged with punishments the scroll,
I am the master of my fate:
I am the captain of my soul.

POEM

LOUISIANA TECH FOOTBALL TEAM (1947-1950)
REUNION 2010

Ah, my dear friends, gathered from far and near
I find it harder and harder to wait an entire year
For us to all be together to let the good times roll
To kick up our heels and reminisce of cherished times of old.

Looking back, we know our era was surely the best
Those bemoaning hard times today cannot comprehend the test
Our generation was put to during our country's darkest hour
But we rallied, won the Great War, and made America the world's
    superpower.

We did not sit back waiting for bailouts, entitlements, piling on debt
    for future years
Our stimulus package was true grit bought with our own blood,
    sweat, and tears.

The news daily predicts that in 2010 the U.S. will sink hopelessly in
    some black hole.
We say, NO WAY, since the year began with our Saints winning the
    Super Bowl.
Did Hell really freeze over? We angels will never know.
But we did have a clue when D.C. was buried in a foot of snow.

Mel Barney

REUNION POEM (continued)

So to all who see doom and gloom as an inevitable fact
We'll just look them square in the eyes and give them a big
         WHO DAT!
For the wisdom we have gained in living well and long
Is knowing our country will prevail and prosper if our people
         stay strong.

And so, dear champions of Tech red and blue,
Once again it seems it is all up to you.
Step forward, go forth, and lead the hale and hearty
Even if it means you macho guys have to attend a tea party.

Remind those who have lost their drive and their nerve
What it's like to sacrifice and serve.
The downs often outnumber the ups, it is true,
But giving in or giving up is never an option for you.

You can teach this millennium generation to hang on tight
And prove once again a bulldog never loses its bite.

Let's now raise our glasses to our incredible, lasting bond
And honor those we love in that Great Beyond.
Nothing can ever take away one of our special band
Can we keep our circle ever unbroken? That's what we mean by
         "Yes, We Can !"

SeSe Holstead, Poet Laureate

TERRAIN FOLLOWING RADAR
B=26 FLIGHT TEST LOG – 227 FLIGHTS

FLIGHT #	DATE OF FLIGHT	FLIGHT PERSONNEL
	5-2-61	Truhill, Barney
	5-6-61	Truhill, Harris, Barney
	5-9-61	Truhill, Harris, DeWeese, Sharp, Walton
	5-9-61	Truhill, Harris, Barney
	5-9-61	Truhill, Harris, Sharp
	5-11-61	Truhill, Sharp, Ticknor, Walton, Harris
	5-11-61	Truhill, Harris
	5-12-61	Truhill, Sharp, Murdock, Moody, Ticknor
	5-16-61	Truhill, Harris, Barney, Czanne
1	5-17-61	Truhill, Walton, Ticknor, Harris, Sharp
2	5-19-61	Truhill, Barney, Ticknor
3	5-22-61	Truhill, Ticknor
4	5-23-61	Truhill, Barney
5	5-23-61	Truhill, Barney
6	5-24-61	Truhill, Barney, Ticknor
7	5-24-61	Truhill, Barney, Ticknor, Chapman
8	5-25-61	Truhill, Ticknor, Walton
9	5-25-61	Truhill, Barney
10	5-25-61	Simmons, Barney, Sharpe, Harris
11	5-25-61	Truhill, Barney, Ticknor
12	5-26-61	Simmons, Barney, Ticknor
13	5-26-61	Simmons, Barney, Ticknor
14	5-27-61	Simmons, Walton, Ticknor
15	5-29-61	Truhill, Walton, Ticknor
16	5-29-61	Simmons, Walton, Ticknor
17	5-29-61	Simmons, Barney, Ticknor
18	6-3-61	Simmons, Barney, Ticknor
19	6-5-61	Simmons, Barney, Ticknor
20	6-5-61	Simmons, Barney, Ticknor
21	6-5-61	Truhill, Barney, Ticknor
22		
23	6-9-61	Truhill, Barney, Zimmerman
24	6-10-61	Simmons, Barney, Slocum, Ticknor
25		
26	6-13-61	Simmons, Barney, Ticknor, Davis
27	6-14-61	Wells, Barney, Ticknor
28	6-15-61	Truhill, Barney, Ticknor, Zasa
29		
30	6-19-61	Truhill, Rubin, Lockwood, Barney, Atkins
31	6-19-61	Truhill, Barney, Harris, Ticknor
32	6-20-61	Truhill, Barney, Ticknor, McCloud
33	6-21-61	Truhill, Ticknor, Barney, King
34	6-21-61	Truhill, Barney, Sharp, Harris
35	6-21-61	Truhill, Harris, Barney
36		
37		
38	6-23-61	Truhill, Barney, Dorsey, Ticknor
39	6-23-61	Truhill, Barney, Strom, Ticknor
40	6-23-61	Truhill, Harris, DeWeese, Ticknor

Mel Barney

B -30
W -23
T -35

FLIGHT #	DATE OF FLIGHT	FLIGHT PERSONNEL
41	6-27-61	Truhill, Barney, Ness, Ticknor
42		
43	6-29-61	Truhill, Barney, Ticknor, Bodle
44	6-29-61	Truhill, Barney, Long, Harris
45	6-30-61	Truhill, Ticknor, Simmons, Barney'
46	6-30-61	Truhill, Barney, Rice
47	7-3-61	Truhill, Barney, Walton, Ticknor
48	7-8-61	Truhill, Barney, Walton, Ticknor
49	7-10-61	Truhill, Sharp, Walton, Slocum, Ticknor
50	7-10-61	Truhill, Sharp, Walton, Ticknor
51	7-10-61	Truhill, Sharp, Walton, Ticknor
52	7-11-61	Truhill, Sharp, Ticknor
53	7-11-61	Truhill, Sharp, Ticknor
54	7-11-61	Truhill, Sharp, Ticknor
55	7-11-61	Truhill, Barney, Sharp, Walton
56	7-12-61	Truhill, Barney, Ticknor
57	7-12-61	Truhill, Walton, Slocum, Ticknor
58	7-12-61	Truhill, Barney, Ticknor
59	7-13-61	Truhill, Barney, Walton, Ticknor
60	7-13-61	Truhill, Barney, Sharp, Ticknor
61	7-13-61	Truhill, Barney, Ticknor
62	7-13-61	Truhill, Barney, Ticknor
63	7-17-61	Truhill, Barney, Walton
64	7-17-61	Truhill, Tucker, Harrington, Barney
65	7-17-61	Truhill, Hansen, Gray, Ticknor
66	7-17-61	Truhill, Barney, Hansen, Gray
67	7-18-61	Truhill, Sharp, Walton, Ticknor
68	7-18-61	Truhill, Walton, Keeble, Ticknor
69	7-18-61	Truhill, Walton, Kassler, Ticknor
70	7-18-61	Truhill, Barney, Gray, Schoenburger
71	7-18-61	Truhill, Barney, Slocum
72	7-21-61	Truhill, Barney, Ticknor
73	7-21-61	Truhill, Walton, Barney
74	7-22-61	Truhill, Barney, Davies, Ticknor
75	7-24-61	Truhill, Walton, Kassler, Ticknor
76	7-24-61	Truhill, Walton, Kassler, Ticknor
77	7-24-61	Truhill, Walton, Kassler, Ticknor
78	7-24-61	Truhill, Walton, DeWeese, Ticknor
79	7-24-61	Truhill, Sharp, Barney
80	7-25-61	Truhill, Sharp, Walton, Ticknor
81	7-25-61	Truhill, Barney, Ticknor
82	7-25-61	Truhill, Barney, DeWeese, Ticknor
83	7-25-61	Truhill, Barney, Ticknor
84	7-26-61	Truhill, Barney, Ticknor
85	7-26-61	Truhill, Sharp, Ness, Walton
86	7-26-61	Truhill, Barney, Sharp, Ticknor
87	7-26-61	Truhill, Barney, Walton, Ticknor
88	7-26-61	Truhill, Barney, Slocum, Walton
89	7-26-61	Truhill, Barney, Walton
90	7-26-61	Truhill, Sharp, Walton

- 2

162

B-26 FLIGHT RECORD

$B-20$
$W \cdot 20$
$T \cdot 18$

FLIGHT #	DATE OF FLIGHT	FLIGHT PERSONNEL
91	7-27-61	Truhill, Sharp, Walton
92	7-27-61	Truhill, Barney, Ticknor
93	7-27-61	Truhill, Barney, Walton
94	7-27-61	Truhill, Barney, Walton
95	7-27-61	Truhill, Sharp, Ticknor
96	7-27-61	Truhill, Barney, Walton
97	7-27-61	Truhill, Barney, Walton
98	7-29-61	Truhill, Barney
99	7-29-61	Truhill, Barney, Ticknor
100	7-29-61	Truhill, Barney
101	7-31-61	Truhill, Walton. Barney
102	8-1-61	Truhill, Walton, Barney
103	8-1-61	Truhill, Barney, Walton
104	8-2-61	Truhill, Sharp, Ticknor
105	8-2-61	Truhill, Walton, Ticknor
106	8-2-61	Truhill, Walton, Ticknor
107	8-2-61	Truhill, Walton, Barney
108	8-5-61	Truhill, Barney, Walton, Ticknor
109	8-6-61	Truhill, Barney, Walton
110	8-7-61	Truhill, Barney
111	8-7-61	Truhill, Ticknor
112	8-7-61	Truhill, Walton
113	8-8-61	Truhill, Barney, Capt. Morton, L.Cdr. Hopper
114	8-8-61	Truhill, Woolson Brown, F. J. Readdy, Walton
115	8-8-61	Truhill, Ticknor
116	8-8-61	Truhill, Barney, Viscove
117	8-8-61	Truhill, Ticknor
118	8-8-61	Truhill, Barney, Walton
119	8-9-61	Truhill, Walton, Majors, Bahner, Wildey, Buwers
120	8-9-61 WASH	Truhill, Ticknor
121	8-10-61 DEMO	Truhill, Barney, CAS, ROD
122	8-10-61	Truhill, Ticknor
123	8-10-61	Truhill, Ticknor
✱ 124	8-11-61	Truhill, Col. Bozeman, Barney, Maj.
125	8-28-61	Truhill, Preston, Dersey, Barney
126	8-29-61	Truhill, Barney
127	8-30-61	Truhill, Ticknor, J. W. McLean
128	8-30-61	Truhill, John Todd, Major – Major George George Adkisson, Walton
129	8-30-61	Truhill, Maj. Gap Haynes. C. G. Johnson Barney
130	8-30-61	Truhill, Ticknor, Burdick, NAA – Col. Miles
131	8-30-61	Truhill, Donald Shaw, Walton, Donald R. Grigsby
132	8-30-61	Truhill, Ticknor, Dove, Kleyla
133	8-31-61	Truhill, Ticknor, Col. R. W. Kersey
134	8-31-61	Truhill, Lt. Col. E. L. Nielsen, Walton Major D. A. Dodge
135	8-31-61	Truhill, Ticknor, Bill Trillo, Don Terrana
136	8-31-61	Truhill, Joele Strange, Walton, Joe Valinski

✱ LOST LEFT ENGINE

- 3

B-26 FLIGHT RECORD

FLIGHT #	DATE OF FLIGHT	FLIGHT PERSONNEL
137	8-31-61	Truhill, Barney, Otto Schoenberger, Capt. Garland King
138	8-31-61	Truhill, Ticknor, Capt. Stephan, ROB. G. Major Niolet, Jam. W.
139	8-31-61	Truhill, Barney, Corky Meyer, Capt. Coates
140	9-1-61	Truhill, Ticknor, Maj. Lytle
141	9-1-61	Truhill, Col. P. F. Quist, OCR&D, C&E Div. Col. E. L. Powell, OCR&D, AM Div. Walton
142	9-1-61	Truhill, Ticknor, Ed Sharkey, (RAND) Col. Rankin
143	9-1-61	Truhill, Major Sugerman, Capt. Hepfer, Walton
144	9-1-61	Truhill, Jim Murphy, Cornell, Jack Ruby, Cornell, Ticknor
145	9-1-61	Truhill, Jack Ruby, Cornell, Barney
146	9-6-61	Truhill, Barney, Walton
147	9-6-61	Truhill, Nathan D. Pingel, Lt. Col. R. Trenkle, Major R. Archibald
148	9-6-61	Truhill, Richard L. Smith, Jack C. Snead, Victor R. Hollandsworth
149	9-6-61	Truhill, Robert E. Kline, Lt. J. Dixon, John A. Pouch, Sr.
150	9-6-61	Truhill, Z. C. Parker, Cpt. J. R. Morrison, Lt. Col. Jos. Jones, Jr.
151	9-7-61	Truhill
152	9-23-61	Truhill, Walton, Ticknor
153	9-25-61	Truhill, Ticknor, Walton, Kessler
154	9-25-61	Truhill, Walton, Ticknor
155	9-26-61	Truhill, Walton, Ticknor
156	9-26-61	Truhill, Walton, Ticknor
157	9-30-61	Truhill, Walton, Kassler, Ticknor
158	9-30-61	Truhill, Walton, Ticknor
159	10-1-61	Truhill, Walton, Barney
160	10-1-61	Truhill, Walton, Ticknor
161	10-2-61	Truhill, J. E. Gray, R. J. Kennedy, Walton
162	10-2-61	Truhill, Kassler, J. Seel, Barney
163	10-3-61	Truhill, Walton, Ticknor
164	10-4-61	Truhill, N. D. Showwalter, Wayne Carver, Barney
165	10-4-61	Truhill, Kassler, Clough, Walton
166	10-4-61	Truhill, Walton, Barney
167	10-5-61	Truhill, N. D. Showwalter, W. Carver, Barney
168	10-5-61	Truhill, Walton, Ticknor
169	10-6-61	Truhill, Ticknor, Walton
170	10-6-61	Truhill, Lt. Col. Robert L. Warner, Walton
171	10-6-61	Truhill, Walton, Ticknor
172	10-7-61	Truhill, Walton, Kassler
173	10-31-61	Truhill, Walton, Ticknor

- 4

B-26 FLIGHT RECORD

B-   11
W-   30
T- 12

FLIGHT #	DATE OF FLIGHT	FLIGHT PERSONNEL
174	11-3-61	Truhill, Walton, Ticknor
175	11-3-61	Truhill, Walton, Ticknor
176	11-4-61	Truhill, Walton, Barney
177	11-7-61	Truhill, Walton, Barney
178	11-10-61	Truhill, Walton, Barney
179	11-15-61	Truhill, Ticknor, Barney
180	11-20-61	Truhill, Walton, Ticknor
181	11-21-61	Truhill, Walton, Barney, Otto Schoenberger
182	11-22-61	Truhill, DeWeese, Springer (British), Ticknor
183	11-24-61	Truhill, Walton, Ticknor, Davis
184	11-26-61	Truhill, Maj. J. G. Bachman, Walton, Lt. Col. Frenchy D. Bennett
185	11-26-61	Truhill, Walton, Barney
186	11-28-61	Truhill, Walton, Barney
187	11-29-61	Truhill, Max. A. Clark, Major; James C. Pike, Major, Capt. Donald Wray Capt. David B. King, Barney
188	11-29-61 ARMY	Truhill, Major J. E. Holstad, Walton, Capt. R. Greenwell
189	11-29-61	Truhill, Charles L. Martin, John Gray, Walton
190	11-30-61	Truhill, Barney, Walton
191	11-30-61	Truhill, A. T. Harbin, GELAC, Dept 72-15 F. J. Overcash, GELAC, Dept 72-15 Walton
192	11-30-61 LOCKHEED MARRIETTA	Truhill, J. K. Walls, (Kermit) J. R. King, B. S. Duggan
193	11-30-61	Truhill, V. Campbell, A. R. Holt, B. H. Watkins
194	11-30-61	Truhill, Barney, Walton
195	12-1-61	Truhill, Major Lolyd Tidd, Barney, Capt. H. L. Hammond
196	12-1-61 TAC	Truhill, Major J. A. Eatherly, Walton, Colonel James R. Wilson
197	12-1-61 LANGLEY	Truhill, Major. T. O. Aultman, Major Miller, Major B. P. Robson, Walton
198	12-2-61	Truhill, Barney, Walton
199	12-6-61	Truhill, Walton, Davis
200	12-7-61	Truhill, Walton, Davis
201	12-7-61	Truhill, Walton, Ticknor
202	12-7-61	Truhill, Lt. Col. Griner, Ticknor, Major Regenberger
203	12-9-61	Truhill, Walton
204	12-12-61	Truhill, Walton, Ticknor
205	12-12-61	Truhill, Barney, Tuttle, (Convair) Major Bernhoff (SPO) Patterson AFB
206	12-22-61	Truhill, Walton, J. Carr
207	12-30-61	Truhill, Walton, Barney
208	12-30-61	Truhill, Walton, Barney
209	1-2-62	Truhill, Ike Lee, Walton, Charlie Young
210	1-2-62	Truhill, Ike Lee, E. Ticknor, Walton
211	1-2-62	Truhill, Walton, Barney, Ticknor
212	1-3-62	Truhill, Maj. Mullem, Col. K. L. Temple, Barney
213	1-4-62	Truhill, Maj. Rust, Maj. Dahl, Ticknor

Mel Barney

$B-2$
$w-2$
$T-5$

B-26 FLIGHT RECORD

FLIGHT #	DATE OF FLIGHT	FLIGHT PERSONNEL
214	1-5-62	Truhill, B Jones, Walton, Ticknor
215	1-8-62	Truhill, Barney, Walton, Ticknor
216	1-10-62	Truhill, Sid Munns (uk), Pat Walker (uk), Barney
217	1-10-62	Truhill, Thorne (uk), Byrne (uk), Ticknor
218	1-11-62	Truhill, Capt. King, Young, Ticknor
219	1-11-62	Truhill, Thorne (uk), Byrne (uk), Ticknor

Plano Star Courier

March 29, 1987

🔹 A Harte-Hanks Community Newspaper

50¢

Vol. 99—No. 195 Plano, Texas

5 Sections

Plano move allows Merit room to grow

By DON MARTIN
Business Editor

Merit Technology Inc., after running out of room for the second time in two years, decided to move to Plano where there is ample room for future expansion, said Mel Barney, vice president of business development for Merit.

The move is one of less than two miles for the military high-tech firm, but its new building at 5068 W. Plano Parkway gives the company plenty of room to grow.

Merit is leasing from Vantage Properties 30,000 square feet of office space on the top floor of the three-story building. By next week Merit will have its name on the face of the new building and a sign in front of the building.

Plans call for the company, with 71 employees, to move from its Dallas location at 1777 Preston to Plano in May.

Barney said the company also based its decision to move to Plano on the building's central location to the company's present and future work force.

Roger Hughes, vice president of finance, worked with a study group to plot where everyone in the company lived and found what location would be central to the majority of the company's employees.

"We want to be in this area because there is such a rich supply of technical people," Barney said.

Barney said Plano city officials were quick to put out the welcome mat when they learned Merit was searching for a new location.

"We were not biased to Plano or Richardson. Either location would have been good," Barney said. "But we certainly have been impressed with the reception that we got from the mayor and the chamber of commerce. They have just been wonderful in helping us. It's definitely been a positive force in moving," he said.

Merit, a two-and-one-half year old company, develops advanced software for military applications. The company also supplies the armed forces with some high-tech hardware, but it does not build its own units and rather works with other companies on a given project, he said.

One of the company's most successful areas is in the development of software for aviation simulations for battle planning.

For example, highly-advanced computer programs developed by Merit enable the military to plan and fly a mission, all through computer simulation. The program will include all the contours of the landscape the pilot plans to fly over,

buildings and structures along the flight plan, the target of the mission and all known enemy battle emplacements, such as radar and anti-aircraft weapons, which will be a threat to the pilot.

The program then will reveal the best route to fly based on the given data. Before the mission, a pilot can practice flying the route. During the mission, a computer on board will help keep the aircraft on the safest course through possible valleys, radar and enemy fire. After it's all over, data from the actual mission will evaluate the mission. The program can even evaluate how well the pilot maneuvers the aircraft because it shows how long the aircraft was open to enemy threat.

Merit works directly with the different military branches and with a number of other defense contractors. Merit's list of customers is a list of "who's who" in defense work. A few of the companies Merit supplies products to are General Dynamics, Bell Helicopter, LTV, Lockheed and Hughes.

Barney said the company recently won three major contracts.

Merit, as a subcontractor to GTE Government Systems, will provide the U.S. Air Force with computer graphics, software, and system engineering to be used in the Air Force's Strategic Training Route Complex. The route system is a mock complex of enemy targets and battle emplacements laid out in the United States, which is used by the Air Force to practice maneuvers.

The company, in a joint venture with SEI Inc. of San Diego, Calif., won an $8.9 million contract with the Navy to install a digital simulation facility at the Naval Weapons Center at China Lake, Calif. The simulation facility will evaluate airborne electronic warfare systems.

The third new contract, coming from Grumman Corp. of Bethpage, N.Y., is paying Merit $2.5 million for work on an advanced radar simulator. The innovative project converts radar images, which may be little more than white clouds on a conventional radar screen, into the topographical landscape being scanned.

Barney said the company has doubled its size in the past year. The bulk of the company's success is tied to the people working for the firm, he said.

"I would attribute our success to having an excellent work force," Barney said. "The idea is to attract the very best technical professionals and give them the latest technology tools to solve military problems."

Barney said the company salary structure is above the market average and operates a strong equity sharing program to keep bringing in the talented people it needs to stay competitive in the defense business.

The company will soon take up most of the third floor of its Plano building, but if the company's growth keeps progressing as it has so far, other floors may soon be part of Merit.

Don Martin/Staff photo

Mel Barney, vice president of Merit Technology, said the defense firm is moving to Plano for more room and the availability of an excellent labor force. The company should start moving to its new building on West Plano Parkway by May.

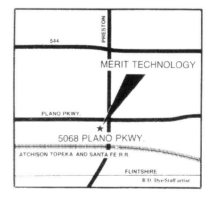

R. D. Dye/Staff artist

167

PATENTS

George Melvin Barney's patents are described below:

United States Patent Office Patent # 3,277,467 (Time Sharing Radar Altimeter);

United States Patent Office Patent # 3,397,397 (Terrain Following Radar);

United States Patent Office Patent # 4,760,396 (Apparatus for setting clearance for Terrain Following Radar System);

United States Patent Office Patent # 4,450,843 (Miniature Biofeedback Instrument);

United States Patent Office Patent # 4,312,358 (Instrument for measuring body functions while exercising);

United States Patent Office Patent # 6,024,713, (Leg support apparatus).

RUSSIAN CLASSICAL MUSIC ALBUM
MUSIC INCLUDED IN ALBUM PRESENTED
TO MEL BARNEY BY MADAM ANODINA,
DIRECTOR OF CIVIL AVIATION (USSR)
IN DALLAS, TEXAS ON DECEMBER 10, 1972

THE CLASSICAL RUSSIAN MUSIC INCLUDES:

The art by F.I. Shalapin (#1)
    1. Slonov - Oh, red sun
    2. Glinka - Ryslan's Aria ("Ryslan and Ludmila")

The art by F. I. Shalapin (# 1)
    8 Russian folklore - Sun rises and goes down
    9 Sokolav - She got noisy, she got stormy
    (about weather usually)

The art by F.I. Shalapin (#3)
    8,9 - Borodin - "King lgor"
    Igor's ARIA. Konchak's ARIA.

The art by F.I. Shalapin (#3)
    1. Alnes - The last trip of a sailor
    2. Malashkin - I wish I could express it in a sound.

The art by F. I. Shalapin (#2)
    1. Giazynav - Vachiche's song
    2. Ryje de Lil - Marselez
    (it's a French hymn as far as I know)

The art by F. I. Shalapin (#2)
    8. Donizetti - Kavatina and Aria
    Don Alfanso ("Lykrezia Bardjia")

RUSSIAN CLASSICAL MUSIC ALBUM (continued)

The art by F. I. Shalapin (#4)
    9, 10 - Boito - "Mefistofel"
    Mefistofel's Aria

The art by F. I. Shalapin (#4)
    1 - Russian folklore - Oh, Vanka
    van, male name)
    2 - Russian folklore - Dybinyshka

The art by F. I. Shalapin (#5)
    1-3 - Mysorgskii - "Boris Godynov"
    Monolog of Boris "I have reached the power"
    4 Rimskii-Korsakov - Fortune teller
    5 Flejie-Horn

The art by F. I. Shalapin (#6)
    1 Klark - Blind field worker
    2 Mysorgskii - Trepak
    8 Mysorgskii - Varlam's song ("Boris Godynov")

The art by F. I. Shalapin (#7)
    1,2 Gyno - "Faust"
    Mefistotel's songs (four lines in each)
    5,6 Mysorgskii -"Boris Godynov"
    Monolog by Boris "Have I reached the power"

ADDENDUM
JACK RUBY HAD U. S. SECURITY CLEARANCE

During our Washington D. C. demonstration flights (page 60), we were flying up to six very dangerous automatic terrain following flights over the mountains west of D. C at an altitude of 200 feet. Grant Dove, Manager of the Texas Instruments Washington Office, scheduled all visitors and checked to assure that they had proper U. S. Security Clearance and a 'Need to Know.' His engineers would then bring them to the airport for their scheduled demonstration flights. This assured that no one would observe these demonstration flights unless they had proper government clearances.

On September 1, 1961 (see flight test log in Appendix, Flights 144 and 145), Ticknor was the TI Engineer on Flt. 144 and on Flt. 145 Barney was the TI Engineer (page 164). To fly on these demonstration flights, the observer had to have a U.S. Security Clearance and a 'Need to Know.' Jack Ruby had these clearances and I recognized Jack Ruby on Flight 145. I do not know when or how he obtained these clearances which were usually controlled by the FBI or CIA.

I became acquainted with Jack Ruby in the late 1950s. As a program manager, I was often called upon to host visiting engineers and managers who solved problems or negotiated contracts with TI. Typically, I would take the customer or vendor to dinner and in many cases entertain them after dinner. A favored spot to entertain these guests (particularly the pilots) was Jack Ruby's Carousel Club. The Carousel Club was a strip club in downtown Dallas. Jack Ruby would usually greet the group and give us a 'good table.'

AUTOMATIC TERRAIN FOLLOWING RADAR LABORATORY

Joe Truhill, Mel Barney, Bill Walton and Hal Ticknor

Our D. C. flight demonstrations were dangerous, scary, and we had a very busy flight schedule. As I was going through the flight logs looking for TI engineers who flew on one or more flight demonstrations, I saw Jack Ruby's name and remembered his flying on two of these flights.

Although Jack Ruby's name appears in the flight log of *FOUR WARS*, I did not highlight the Addendum information about his U. S. Security Clearance requirement until the third printing. Copies of this Addendum are available at no charge to those who purchased an earlier edition by contacting barney.mel@gmail.com.